New Leaf Motif
COLORING FOR ADULTS
Book One

A Day at the Zoo

Krystine Kercher

A special thanks to Christine M. Miller Ramey for contributing
her coloring skills for the cover of this book!

The photos these drawings are based on were taken at

the Henry Doorly Zoo in Omaha, Nebraska
the Menominee Park Zoo in Oshkosh, Wisconsin
the Pioneers Park Nature Center outside of Lincoln, Nebraska
by Lake Michigan on the Upper Peninsula
at Holmes Lake Park in Lincoln, Nebraska
in a local homeowner's yard.

Published in the U.S.A.

Dear artist friends,

Because of the subject matter, and in an attempt to show animals in as natural a zoo setting as possible, some designs in this book are more detailed and complicated than others.

If you're looking for ideas on how best to color these images, the original color photos that I used for design inspiration are posted on **http://creativeindiedesigns.com**.

I recommend using less detailed designs to practice shading techniques, or as a break between more complicated coloring challenges.

When coloring the more detailed designs, it may help to take frequent breaks and tackle one section or one design element at a time.

I suggest using a ruler and a straight edge razor or box cutter to remove the cover and spine for ease of coloring at the top of each design.

Last but not least, there is no 'right' or 'wrong' way to color these images!

I hope you will share your finished and autographed designs with your friends and with me!

I would love to see pictures! Please feel free to share your artwork with me on Facebook at http://facebook.com/creativeindiedesigns.

I hope you will enjoy this visit to the zoo, and have a lot of fun coloring these images!

Blessings,

Krystine Kercher

Table of Contents

Around the Zoo

There are a number of creatures seen about the zoo which don't fit into any specific exhibit!

These animals might be wild, like squirrels, turtles, and ducks, or they might be partially domesticated, like swans and peacocks.

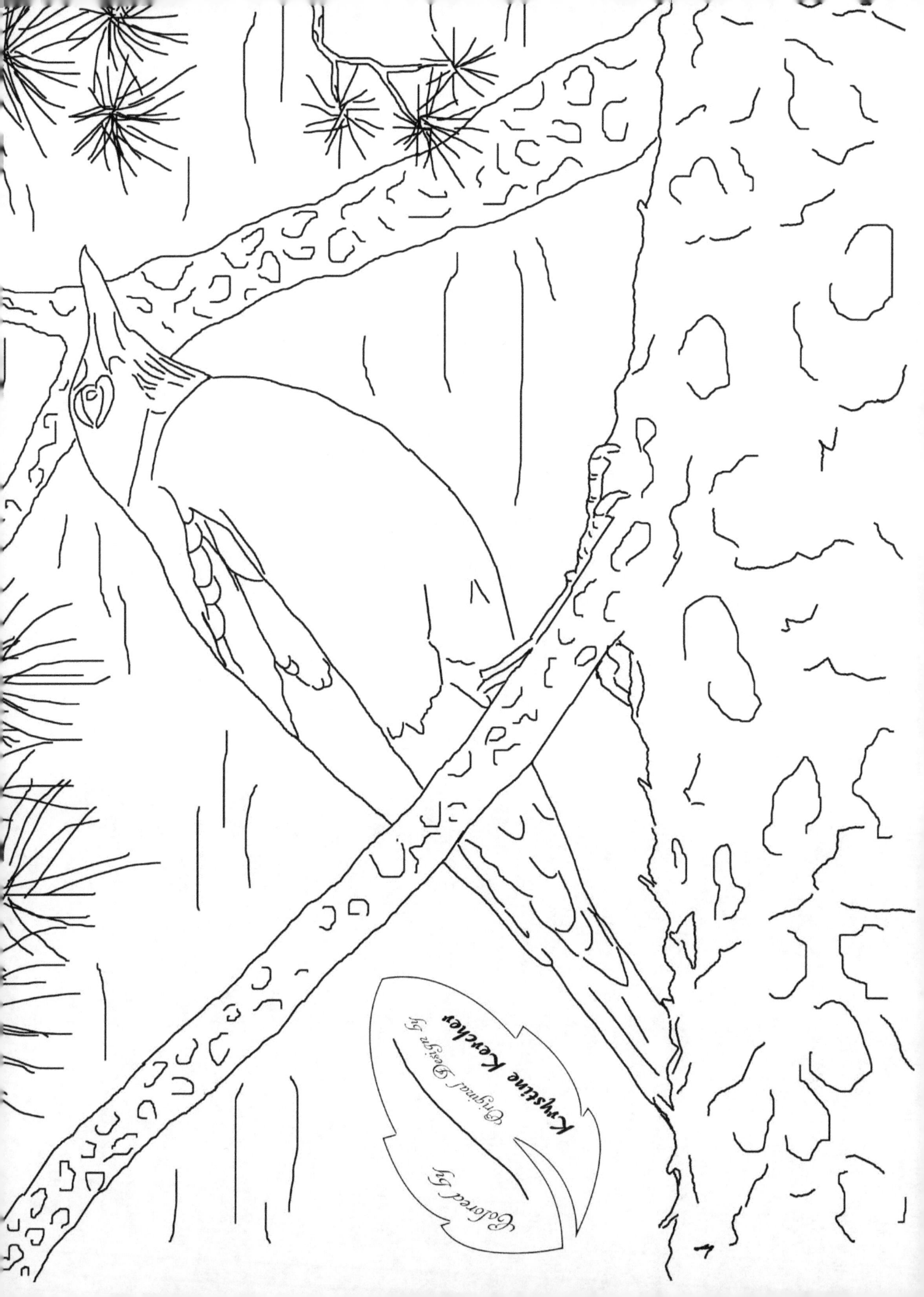

1 - American Robin

We always know that spring is just around the corner when we see the robins flocking.

While zoos don't typically keep robins in their exhibits, during warmer months they can be seen flitting about between the outdoor exhibits.

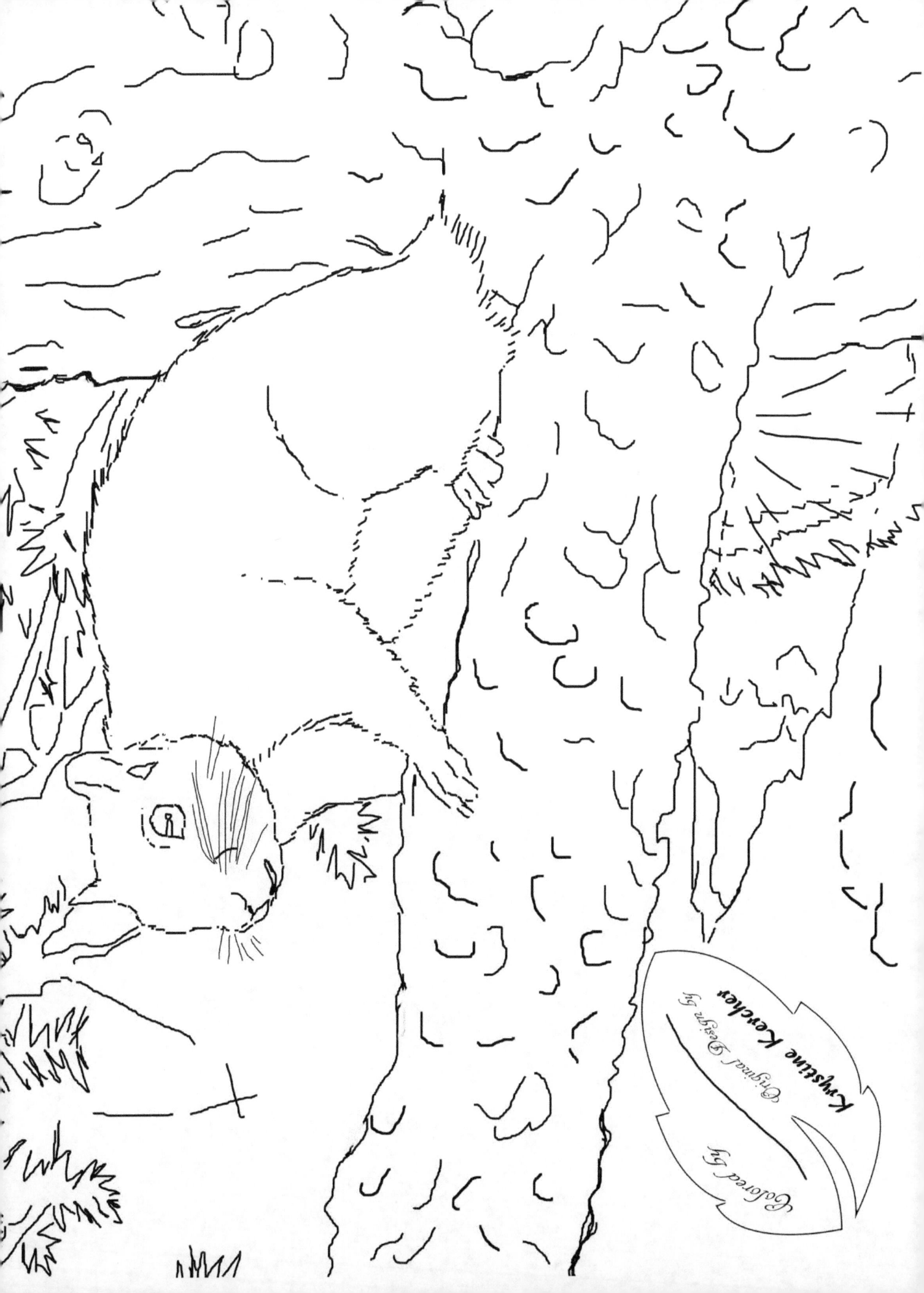

Krystine Kercher
Original Design by

Colored by

2 - Western Gray Squirrel

Squirrels can be found wherever there are plenty of trees filled with their favorite foods. Squirrels eat acorns, pine seeds, sunflower seeds, and other types of nuts. They will also eat pumpkins and corn from squirrel feeders.

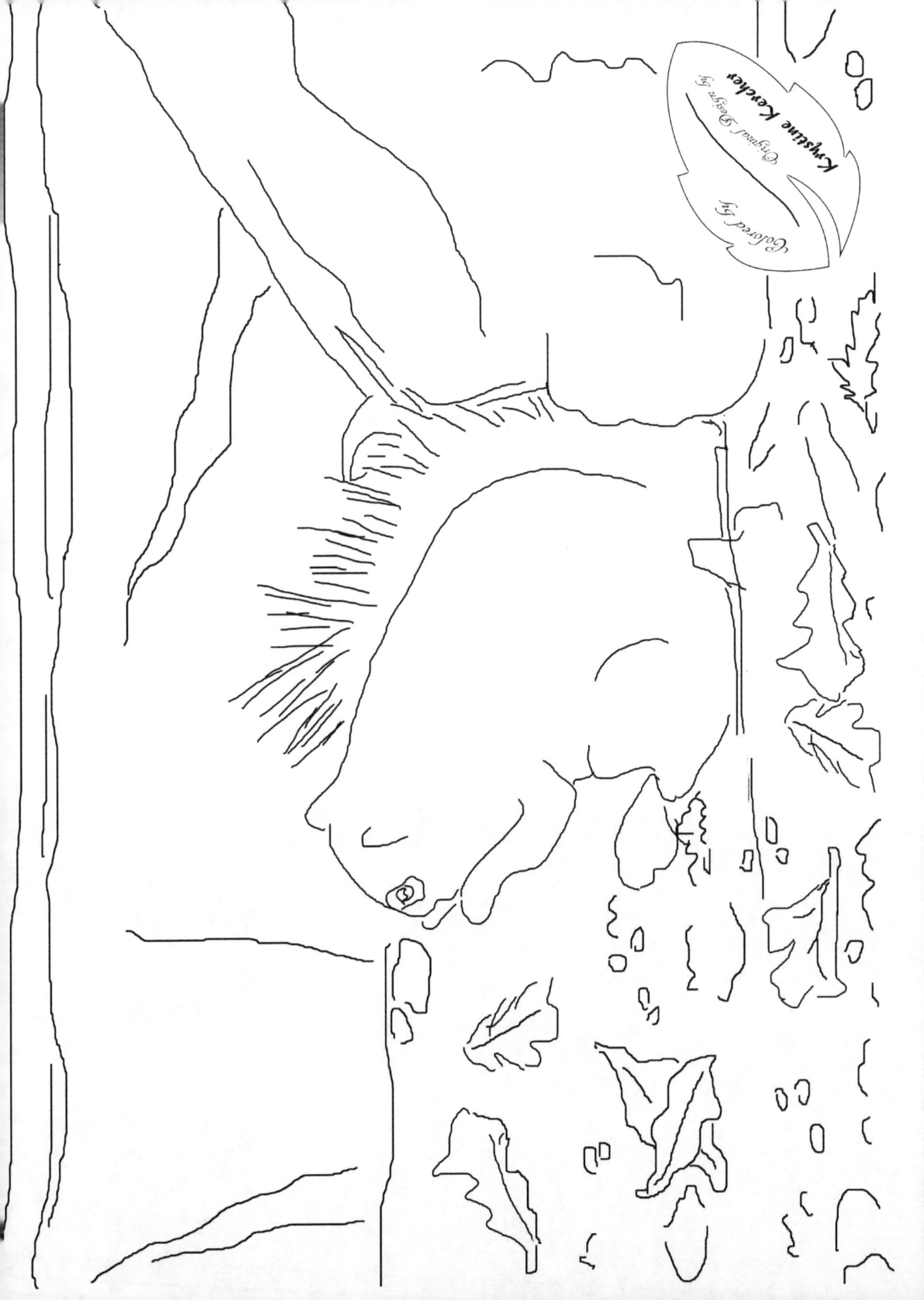

3 - Black Squirrel

This particular squirrel happened to be black as charcoal.

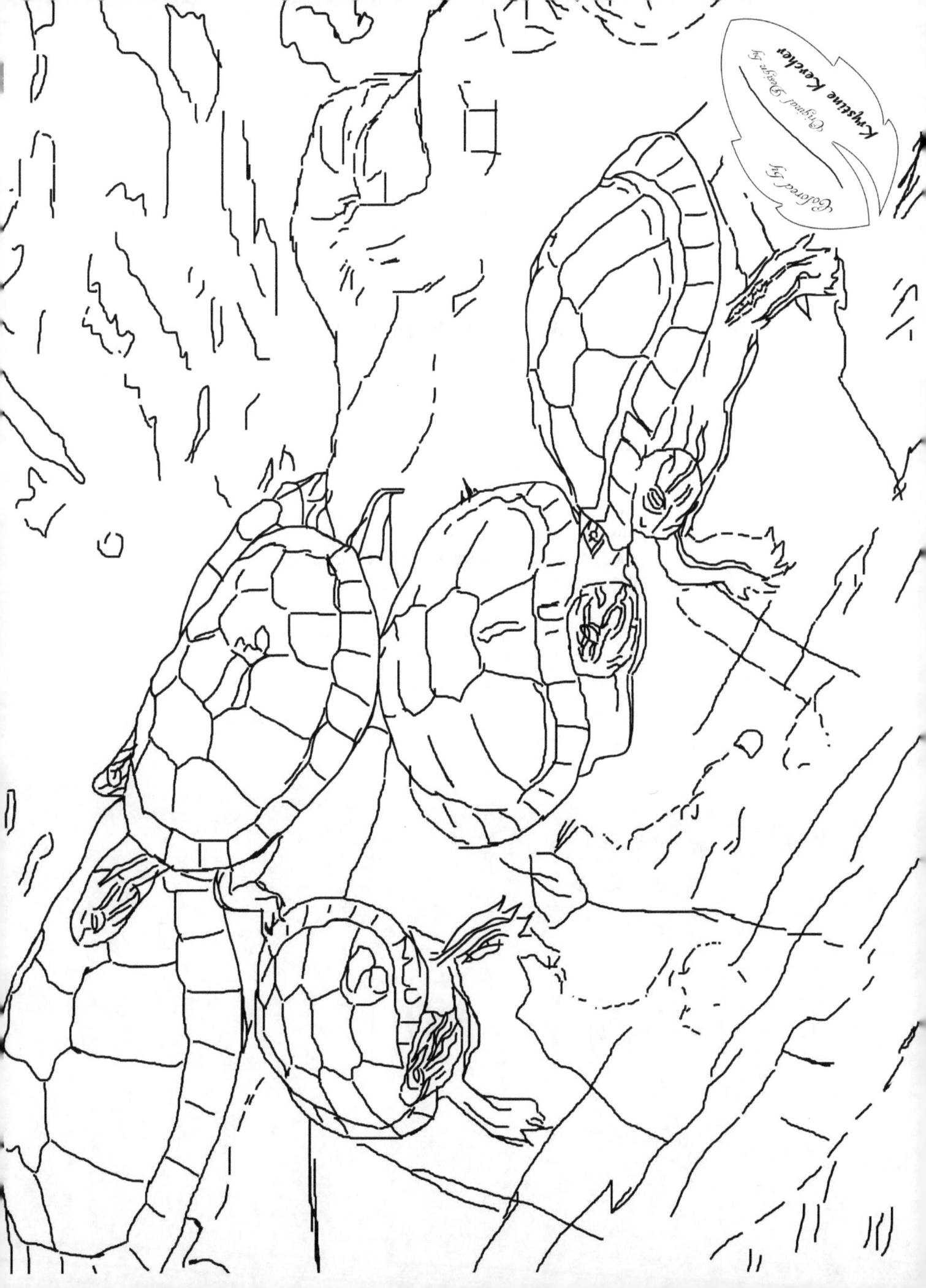

4 - Western Painted Turtles

These turtles might be a little tricky, so I've included a practice page.

These colorful turtles have yellow stripes running down the sides of the cheeks and down their legs. The front edge of each lower shell is a vivid salmon pink.

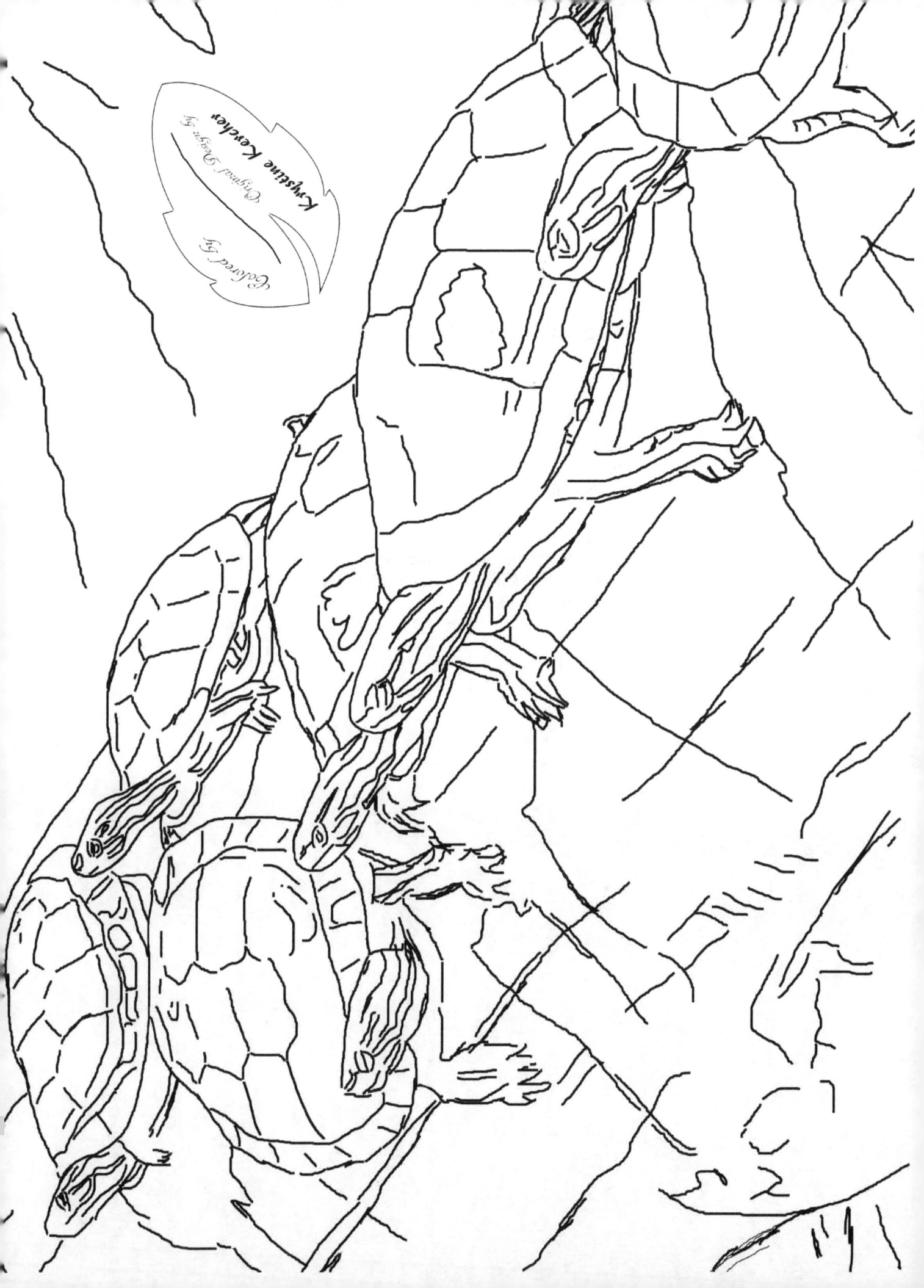

5 - Western Painted Turtles

Western painted turtles can be found sunning themselves on a log in a pond on any warm day, but they hibernate in winter.

These colorful turtles have yellow stripes running down the sides of the cheeks and down their legs. The front edge of each lower shell is a vivid salmon pink.

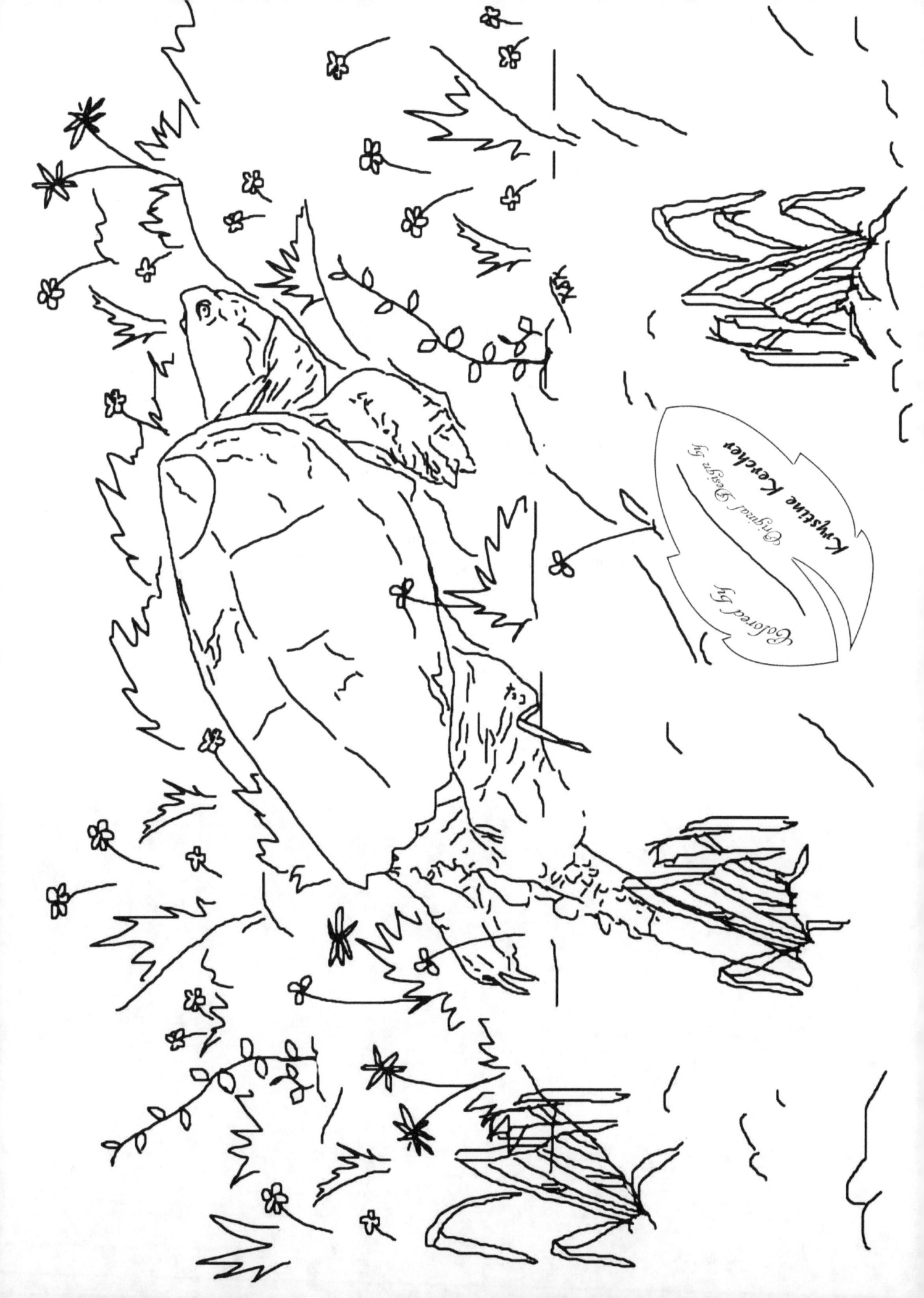

Colored by
Original Design by
Krystine Kercher

6 - Snapping Turtle

What I like best about snapping turtles is how they have such neat tails with dragon-like spikes and scales!

This fantastical creature inspired me to give him a more exciting setting than the one I found him in.

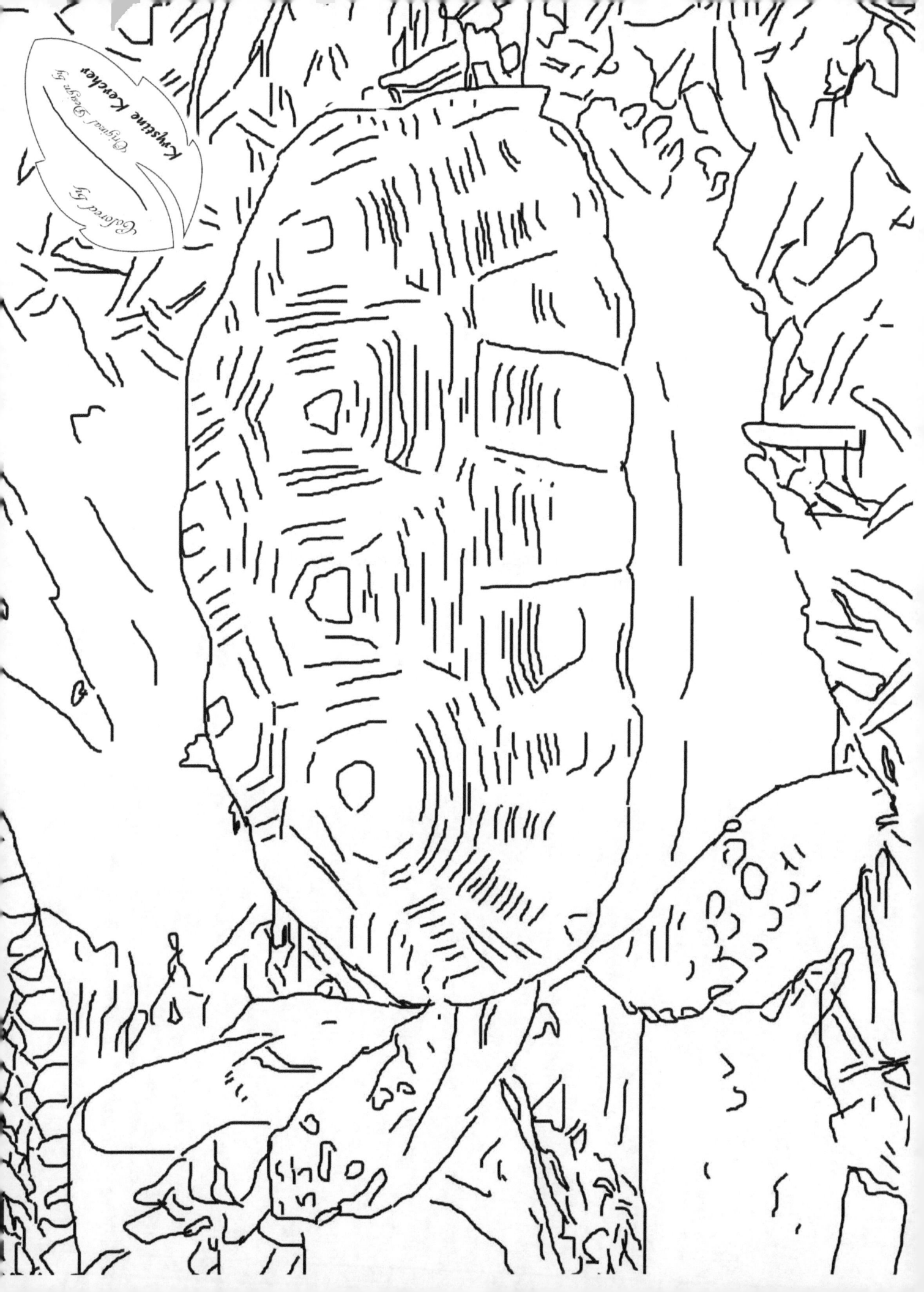

7 - Tortoise

This tortoise is a fairly big fellow who has already lived a lot of years. He seems pretty friendly too!

The interesting pattern in the upper left corner of this design is the back of a black and yellow python sunning himself on the other side of the enclosure.

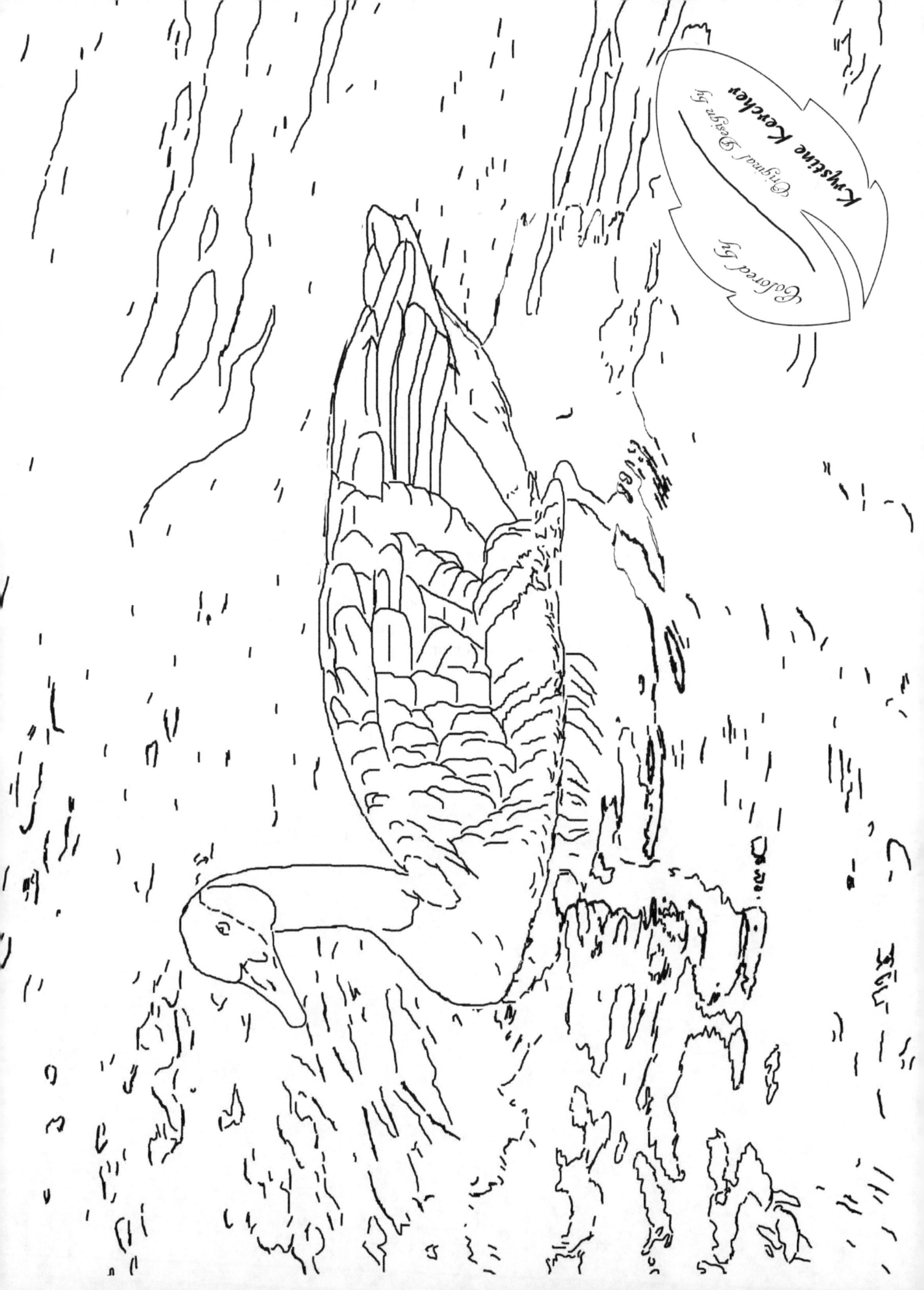

8 - Canadian Goose

Canadian geese are so common, they can be found grazing on plants near almost any pond or body of water.

When not feeding, they can often be found enjoying the water with other geese and ducks.

What's special about this goose is the way the water ripples likes silk around him while still reflecting his gorgeous plumage.

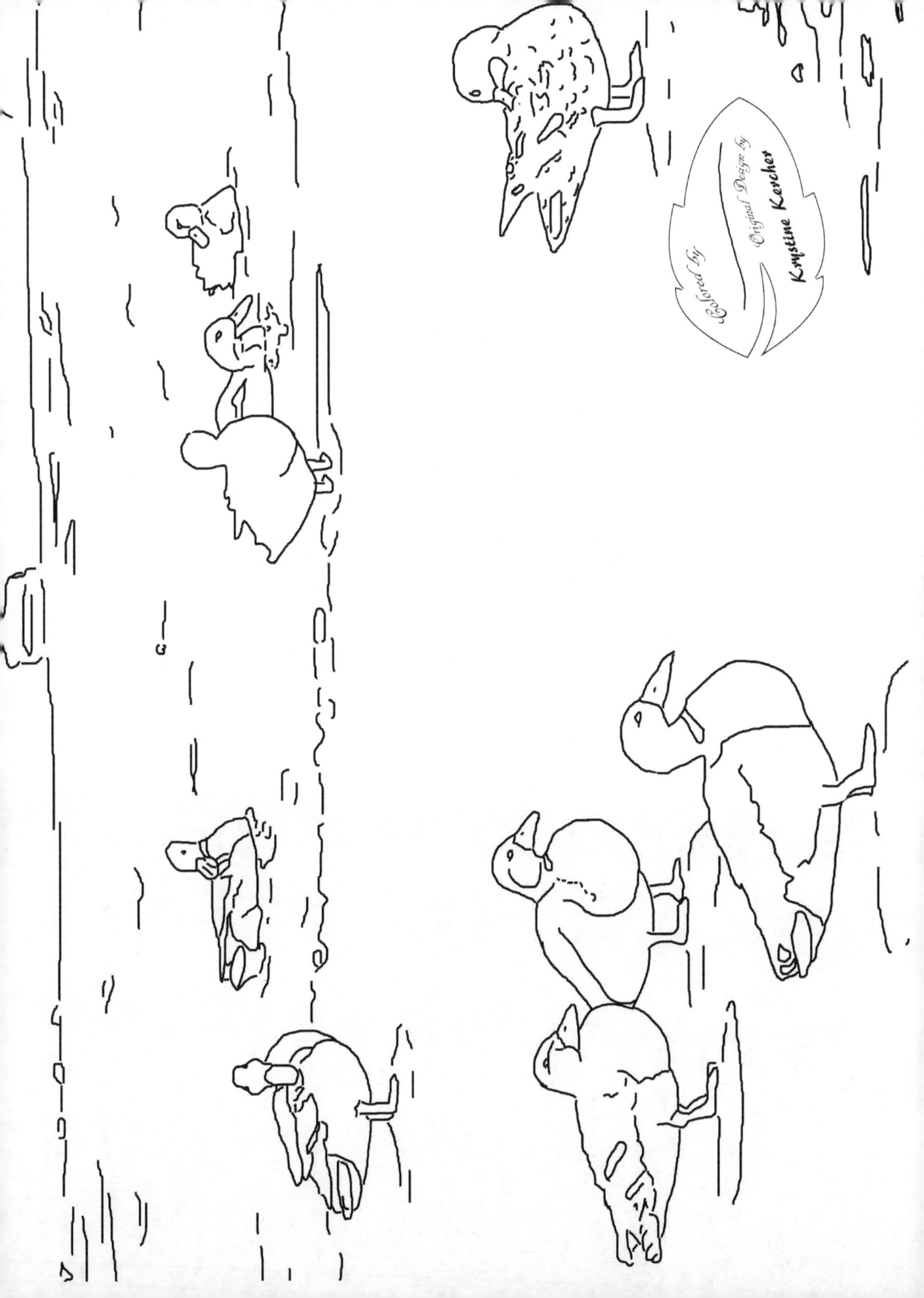

9 - Mallard Ducks

Mallard ducks are so cute how they pair off with the colorful male ducks hanging out with their brown females!

I photographed these ducks at the end of winter while there was still a lot of ice on the lake.

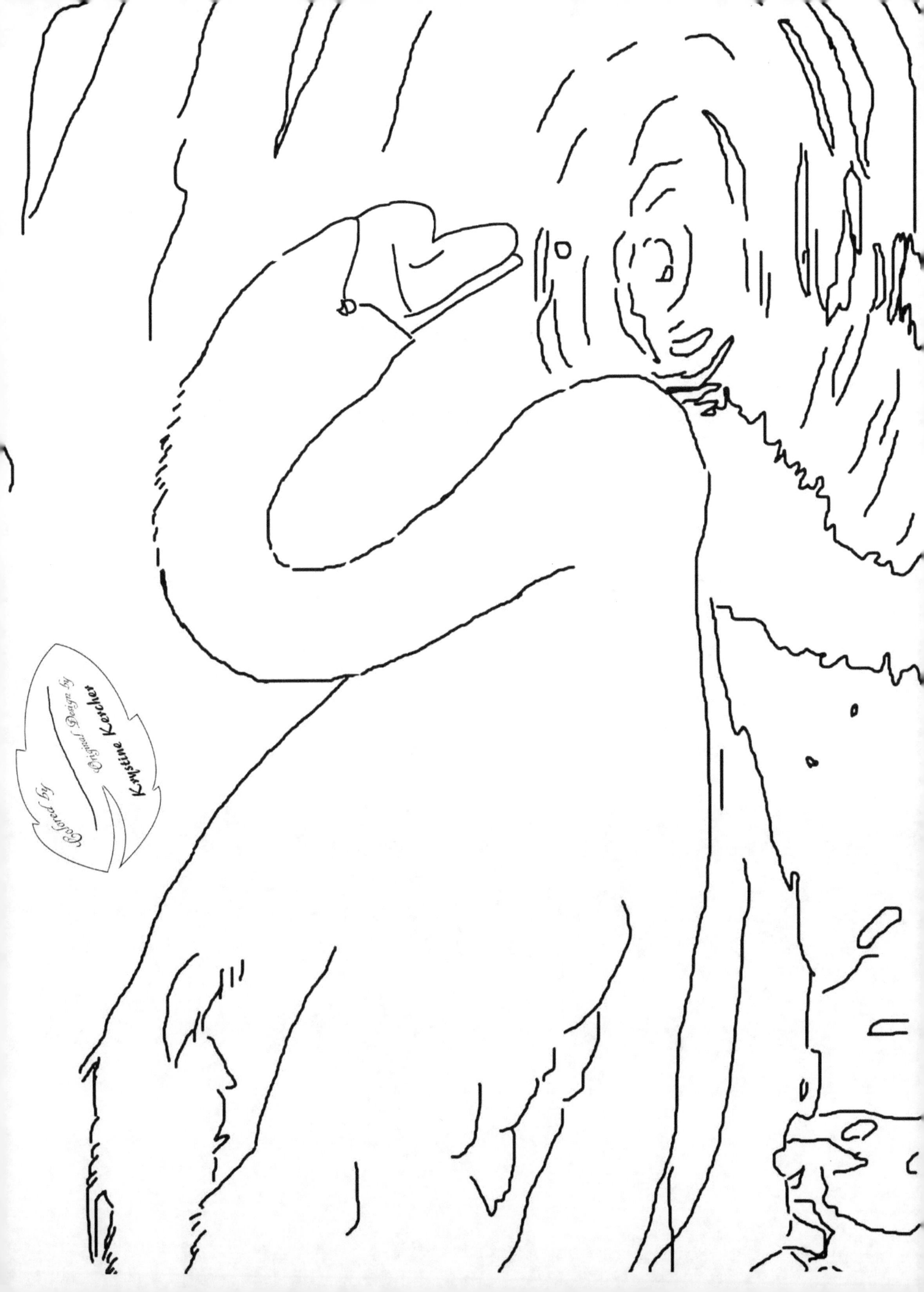

10 - Mute Swan

Is there any bird that is more graceful than a swan? This mute swan is white.

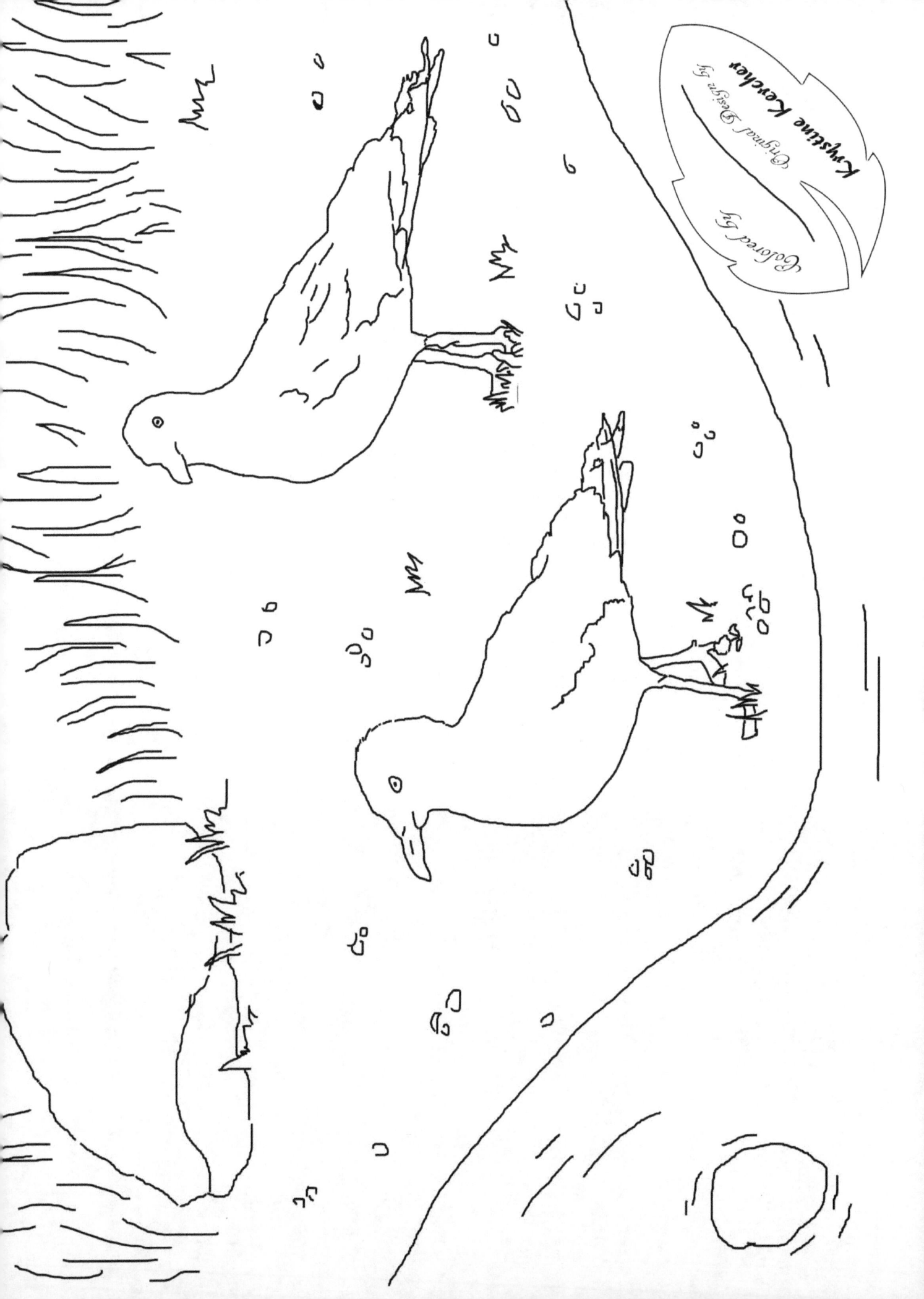

11 - Seagulls

While seagulls can be frequently found near bodies of water, they're also opportunists which can be found flying far inland to feast on grasshoppers and locusts, and French fries dropped in mall parking lots.

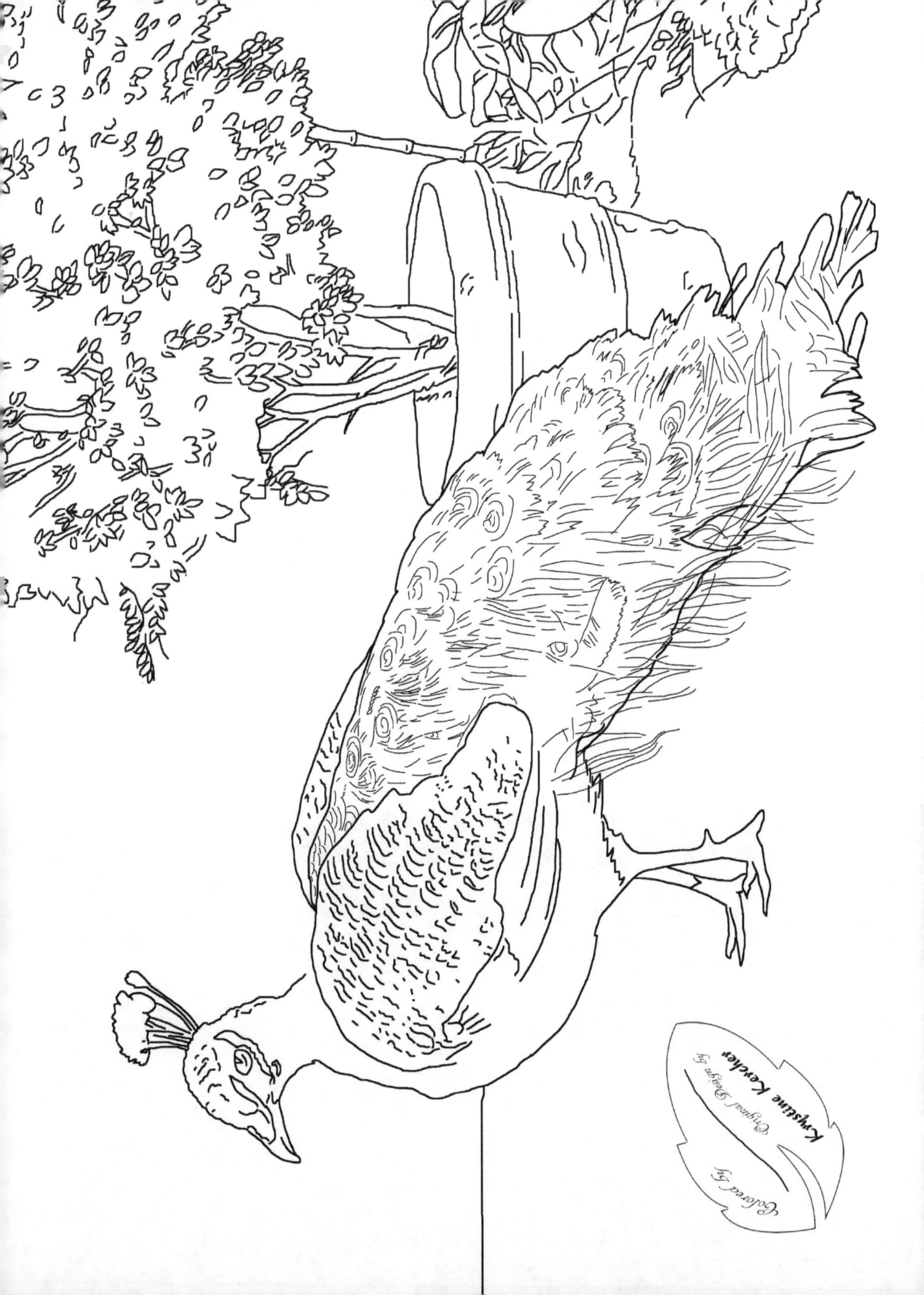

12 - Peacocks

Peacocks and their dowdy brown peahens can be seen walking the zoo grounds except when the temperatures grow too frosty.

I photographed this handsome fellow in strong sunlight with the shadows falling toward me and to the right.

A Visit To The Petting Zoo

Next, we're going to visit the petting zoo.

In the petting zoo are located a selection of domesticated animals that are friendly and willing to let children pet and feed them.

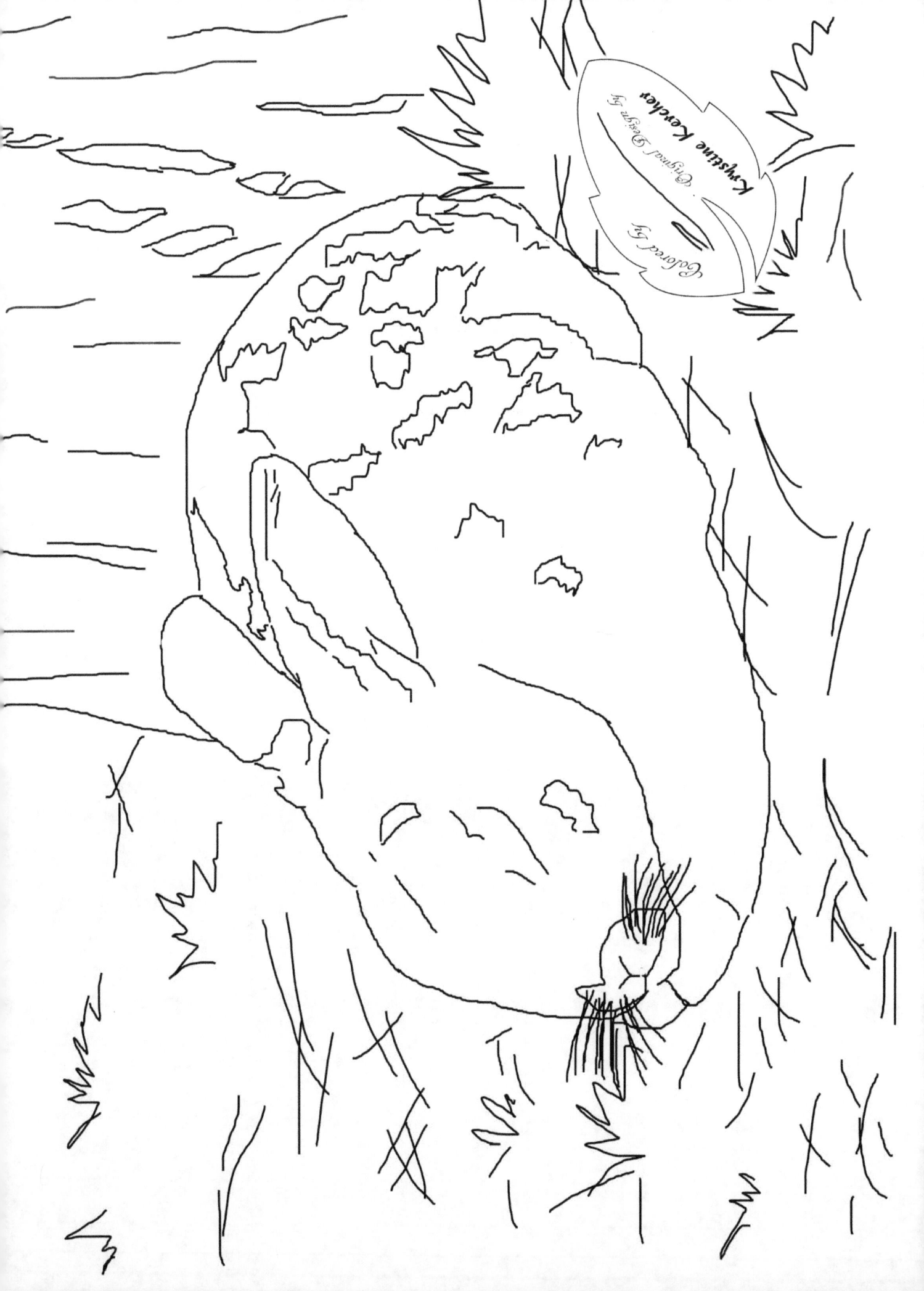

13 - Rabbit

No petting zoo is complete without at least one rabbit.

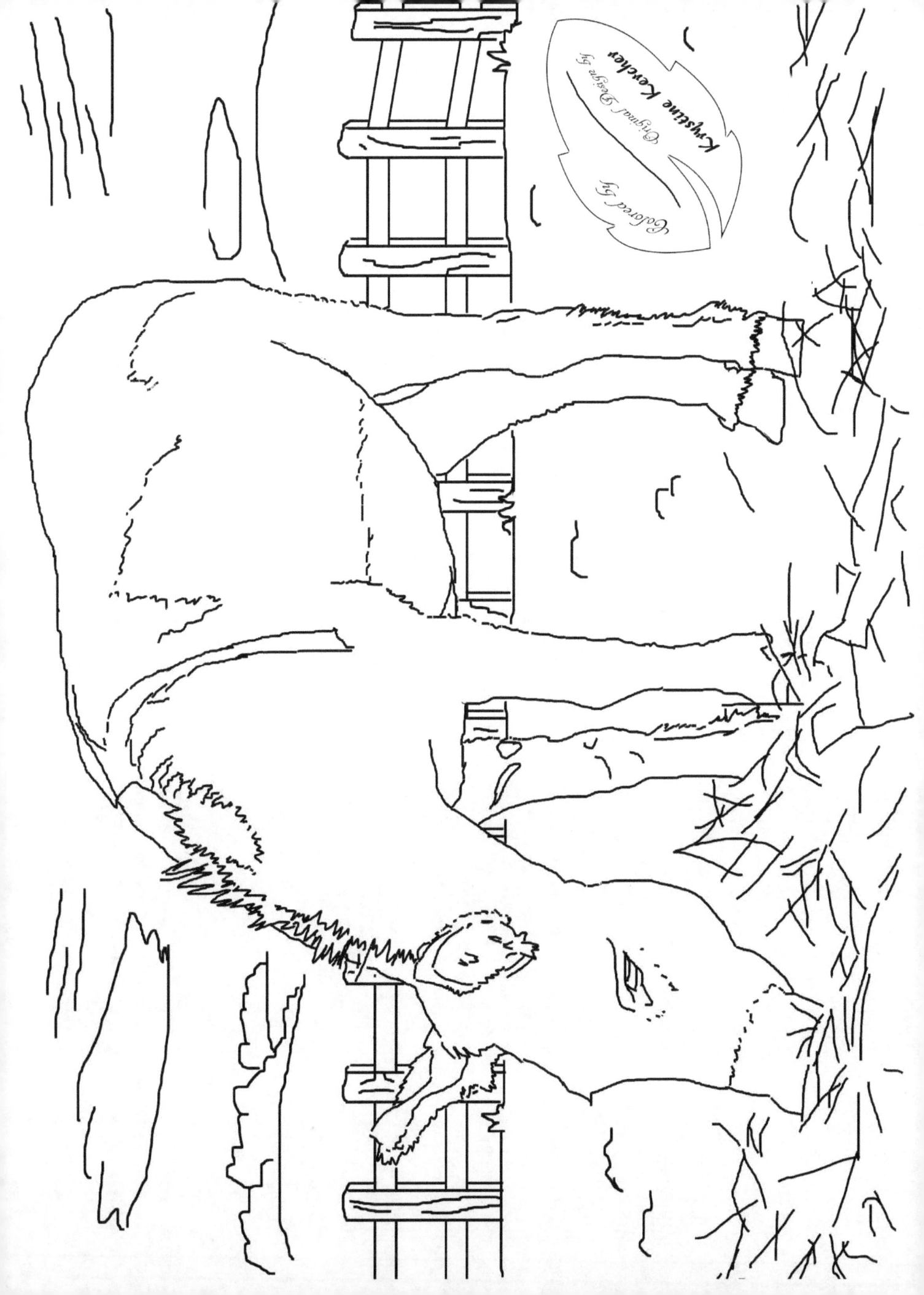

Original Design by **Krystine Kercher**

Colored by

14 - Donkey

Donkeys can sometimes be ridden as well as petted and fed, and make a great addition to any petting zoo.

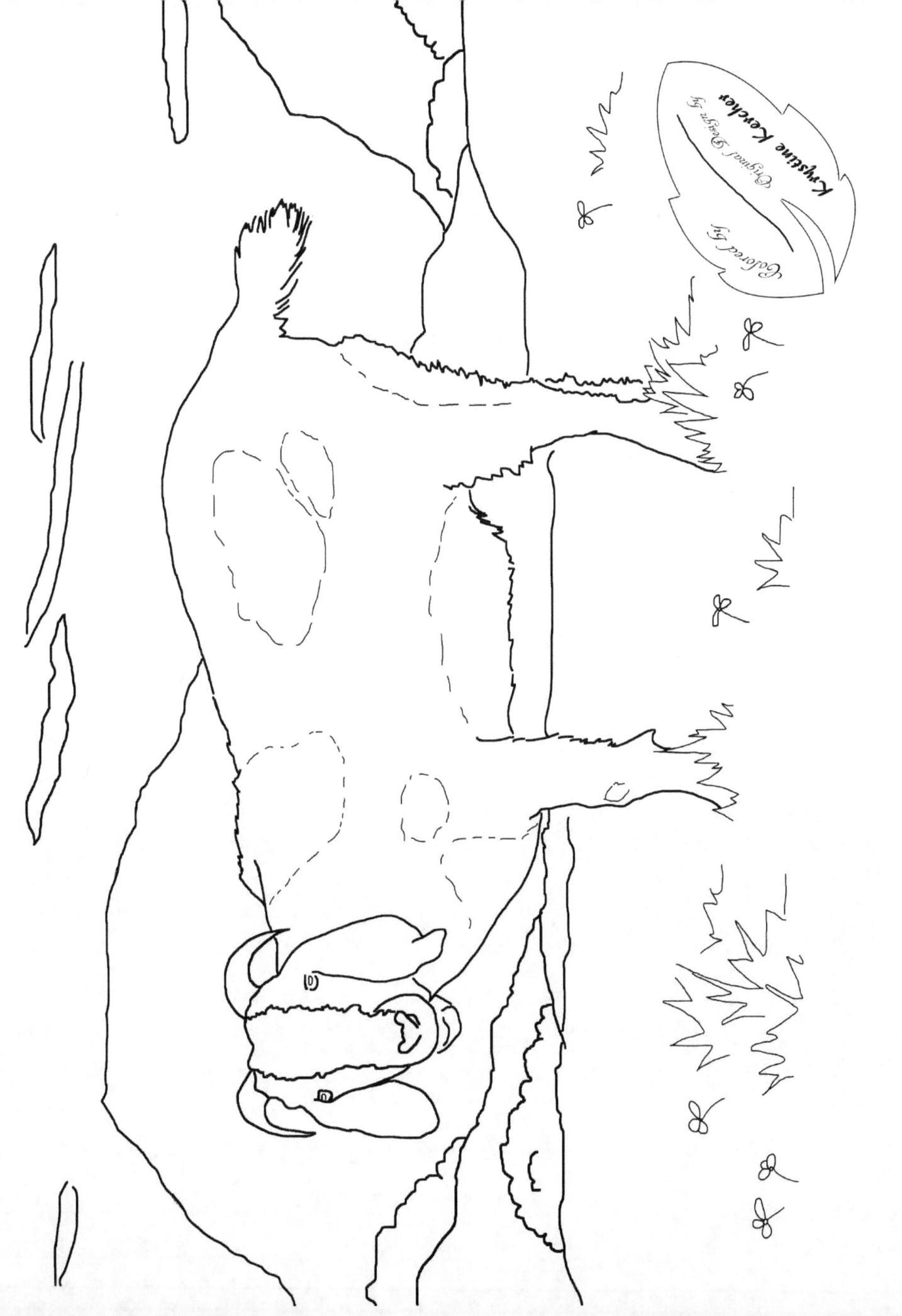

15 - Nanny Goat

In most breeds of goats, the nannies don't have horns, but this nanny does! She's still very sweet.

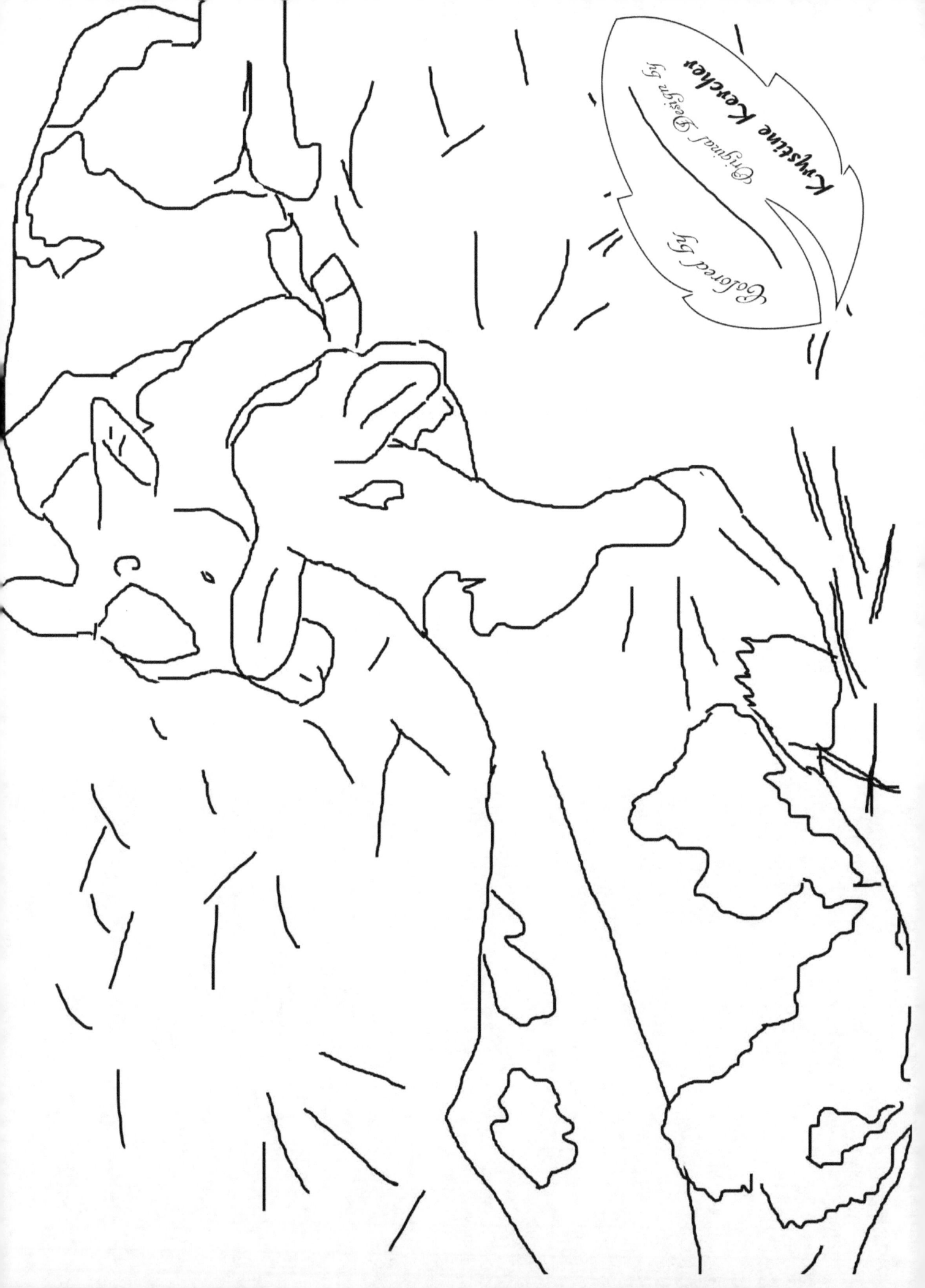

16 - Cows

We also found these sweet calves in the petting zoo.

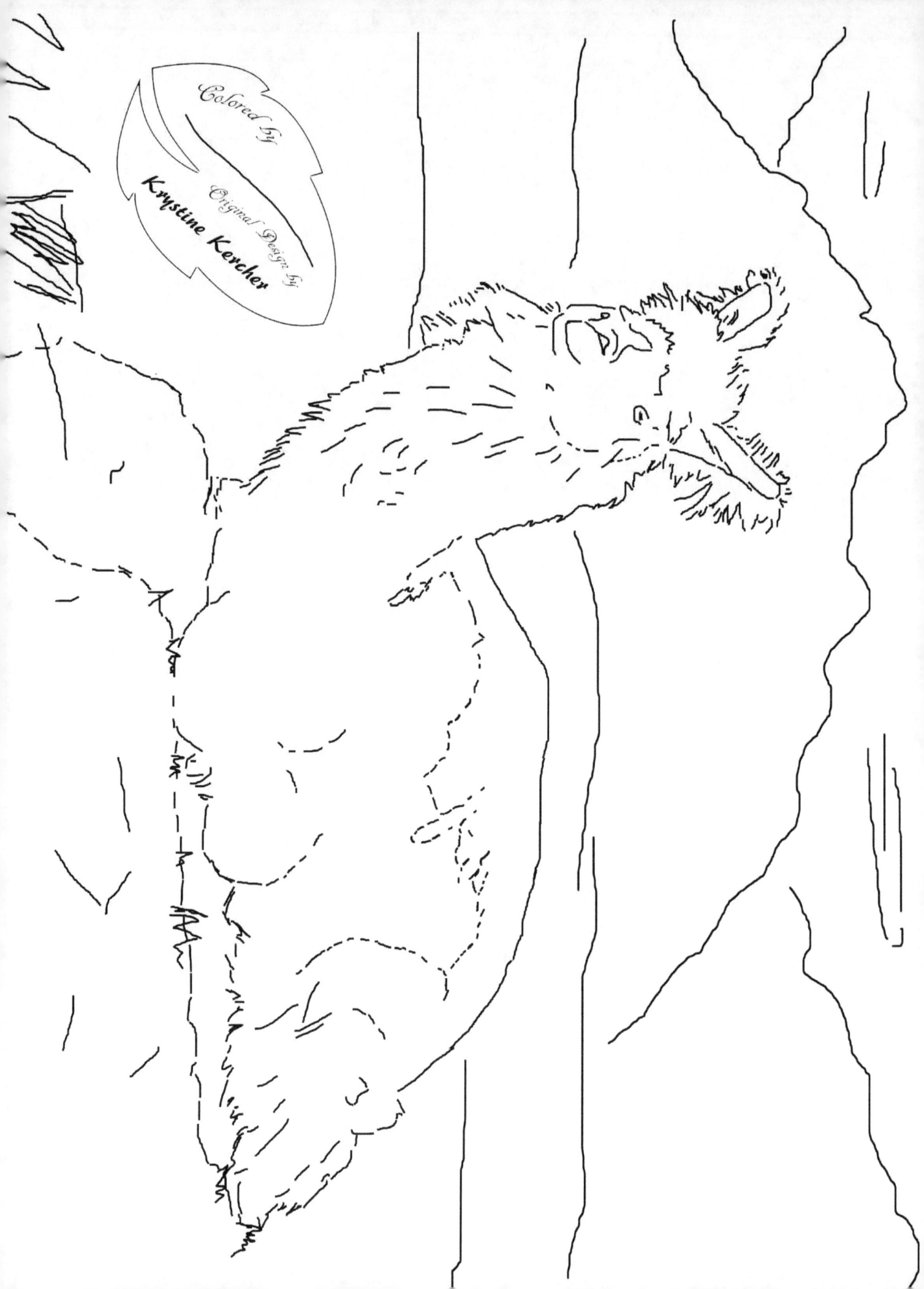

Colored by

Original Design by

Krystine Kercher

17 - Llama

Llamas can be really friendly and sweet, but this llama was tired and hot, and just wanted to take a nap!

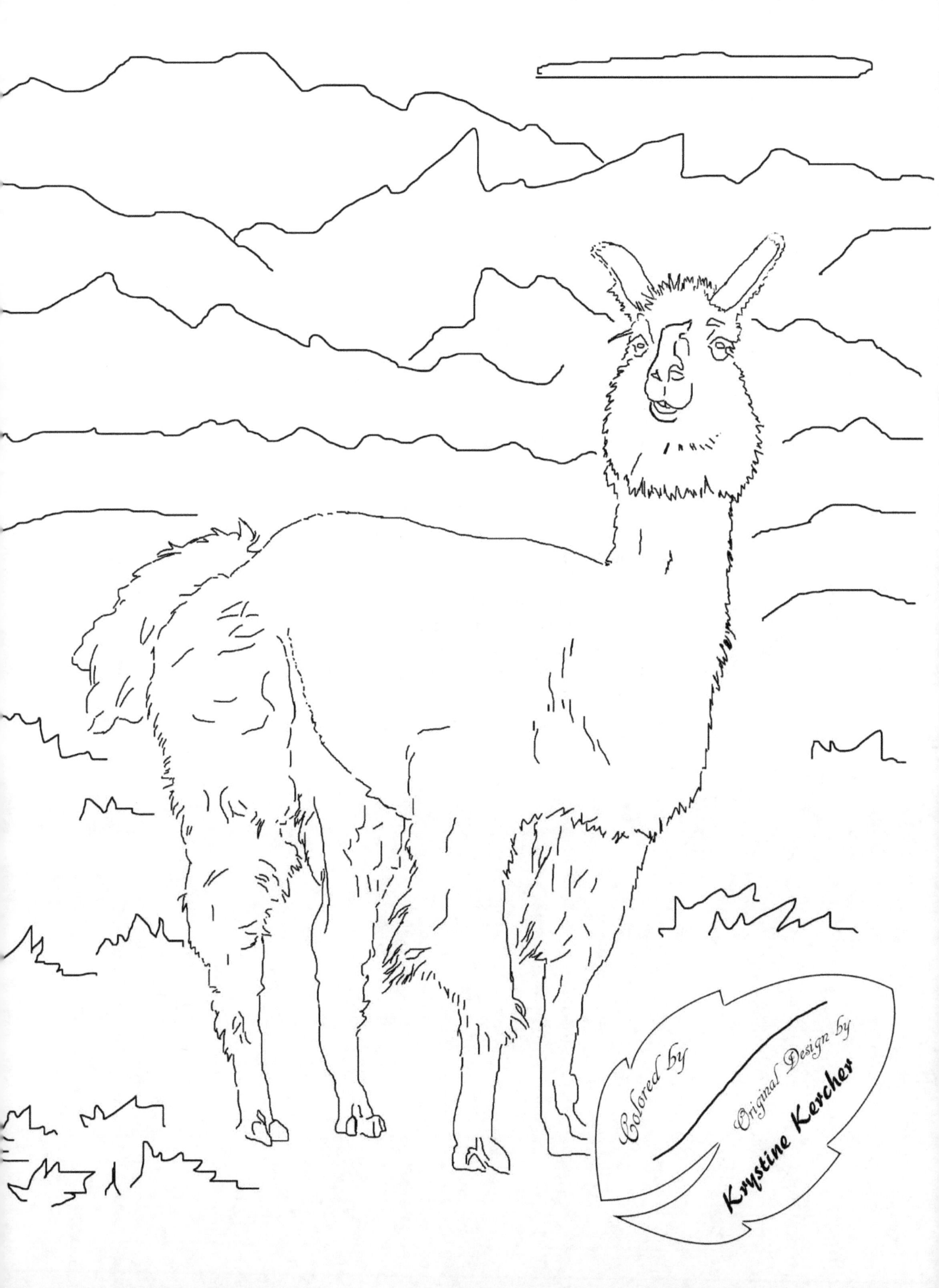

Colored by

Original Design by

Krystine Kercher

18 - Llama

Llamas are very useful animals!

They are used sometimes to guard sheep in the western United States. A full grown llama is able to chase off a coyote or a bobcat, and even a mountain lion!

Llama wool is spun into super-soft yarn, and used for knitting and weaving beautiful clothing!

Llamas are also used as pack animals in the Andes Mountains of South America.

Animals of North and South America

Next, we're off to see animals from North and South America.

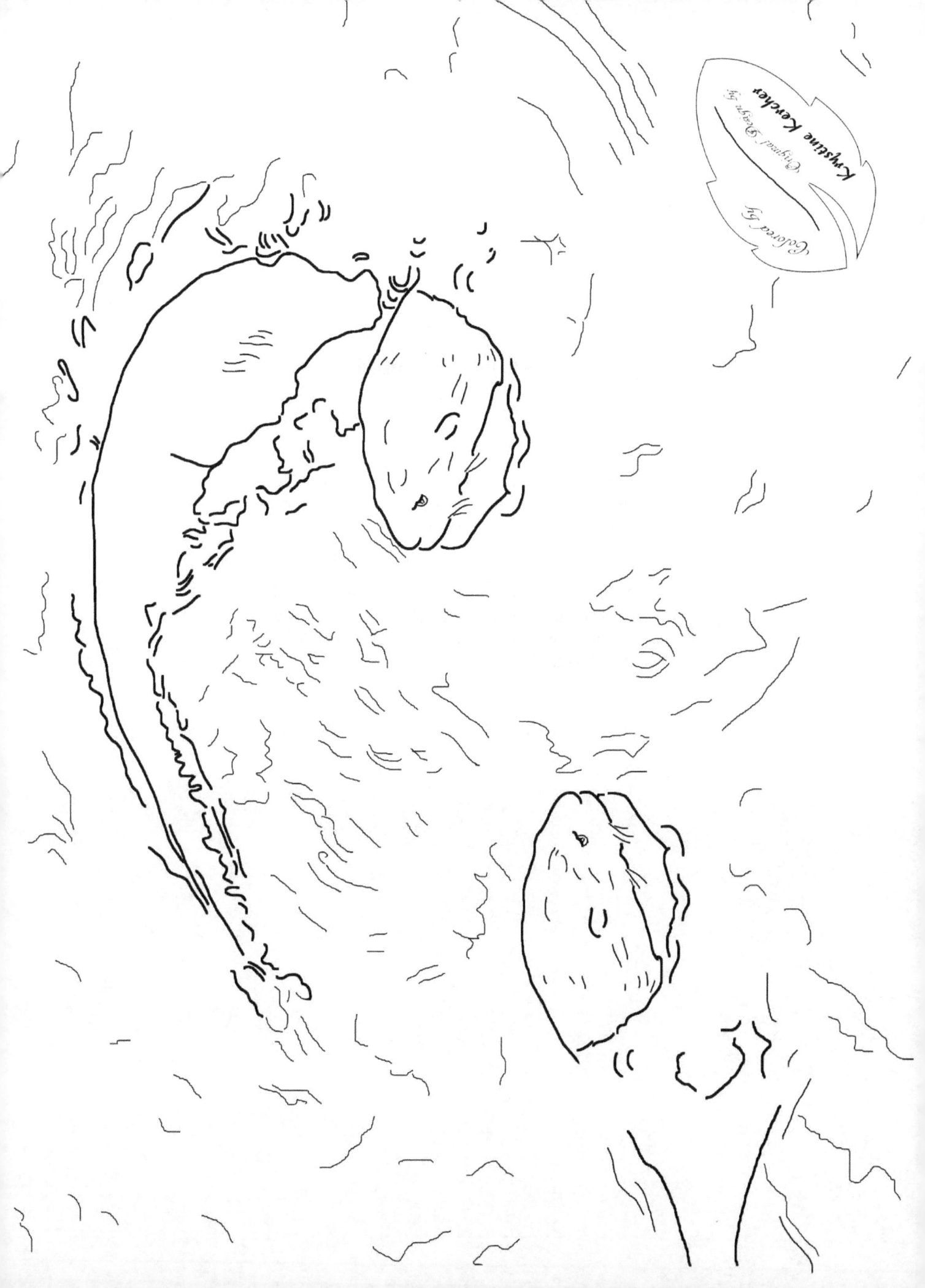

19 - Otters Swimming

Otters are so graceful and sleek in the water! I had the most difficult time catching them moving slowly enough that the photographs wouldn't blur.

What's special about this design is the opportunity to play with light reflections on the water, as well as the waves and froth created by the playful otters.

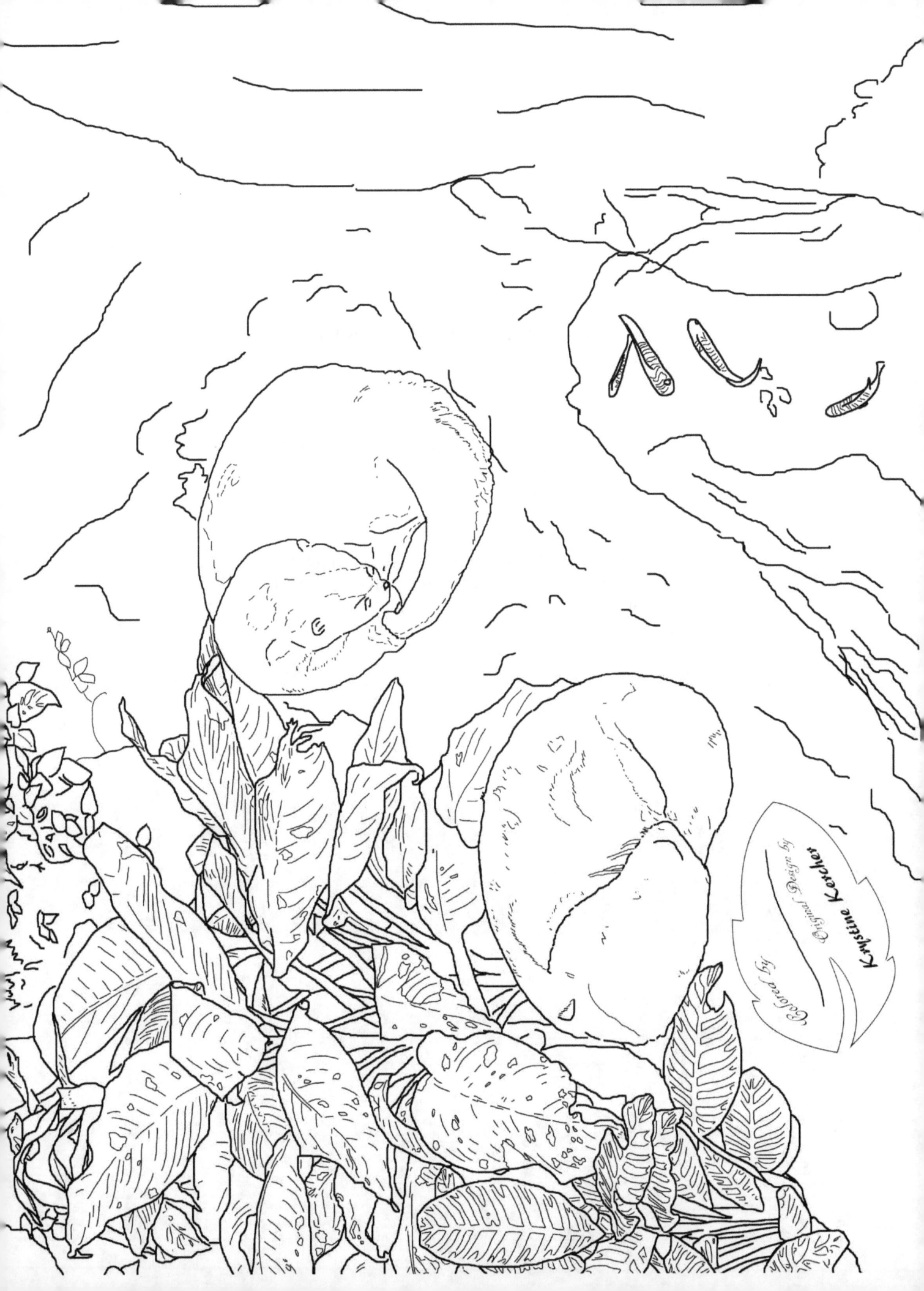

20 - Let Sleeping Otters Lie

Otters have soft, thick, beautiful fur which looks really gorgeous, and it's tempting to try to pet them when they're dry, but they do not trust humans!

It's important to remember that wild creatures can bite when they feel cornered or threatened, even at the zoo.

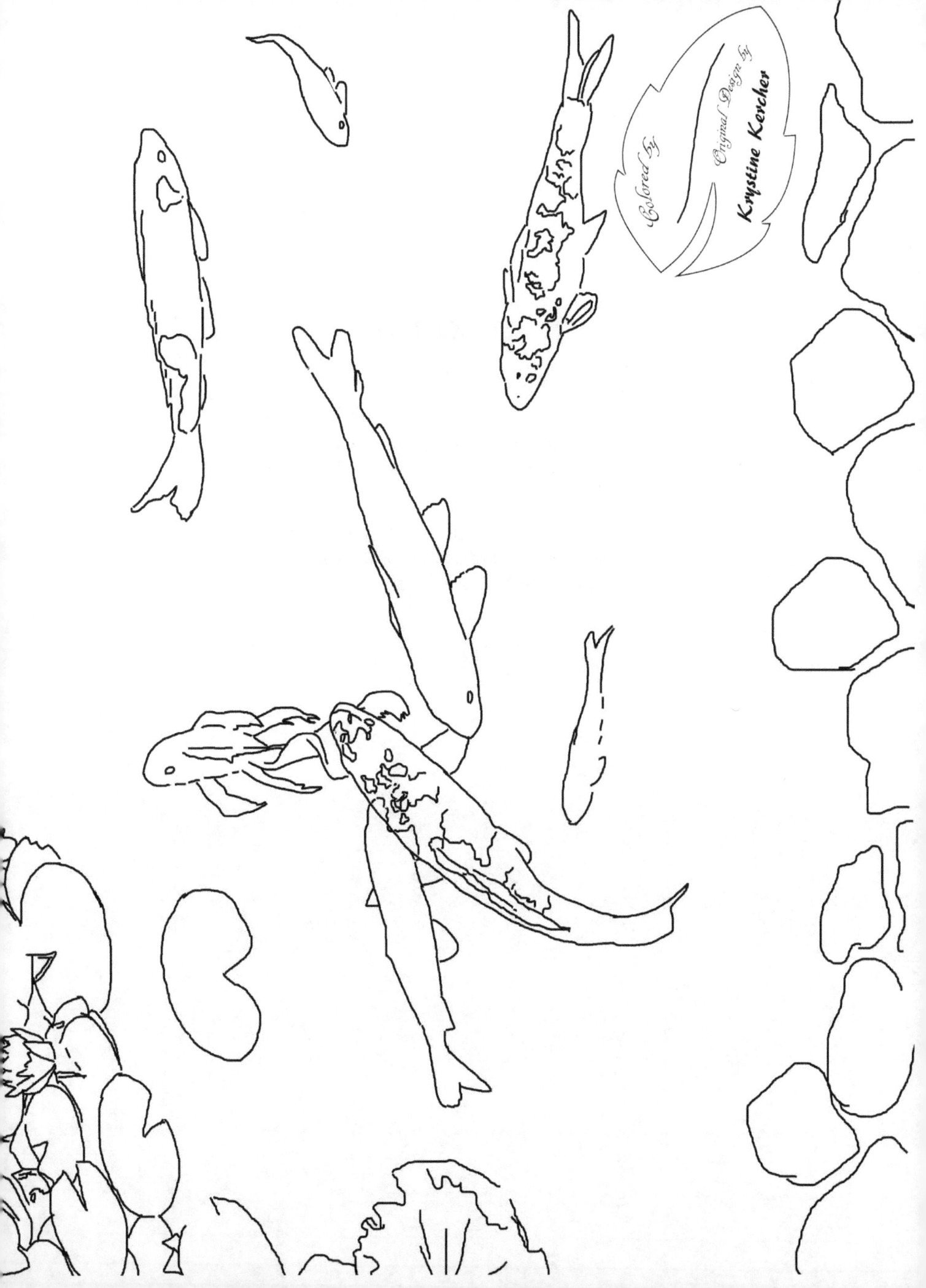

21 - Koi Fish

Colorful koi fish are originally from China, but are now raised in lakes and ponds all over the world.

These koi come in shades of golden yellow, orange, black, and white, but you can color them any way that tickles your fancy.

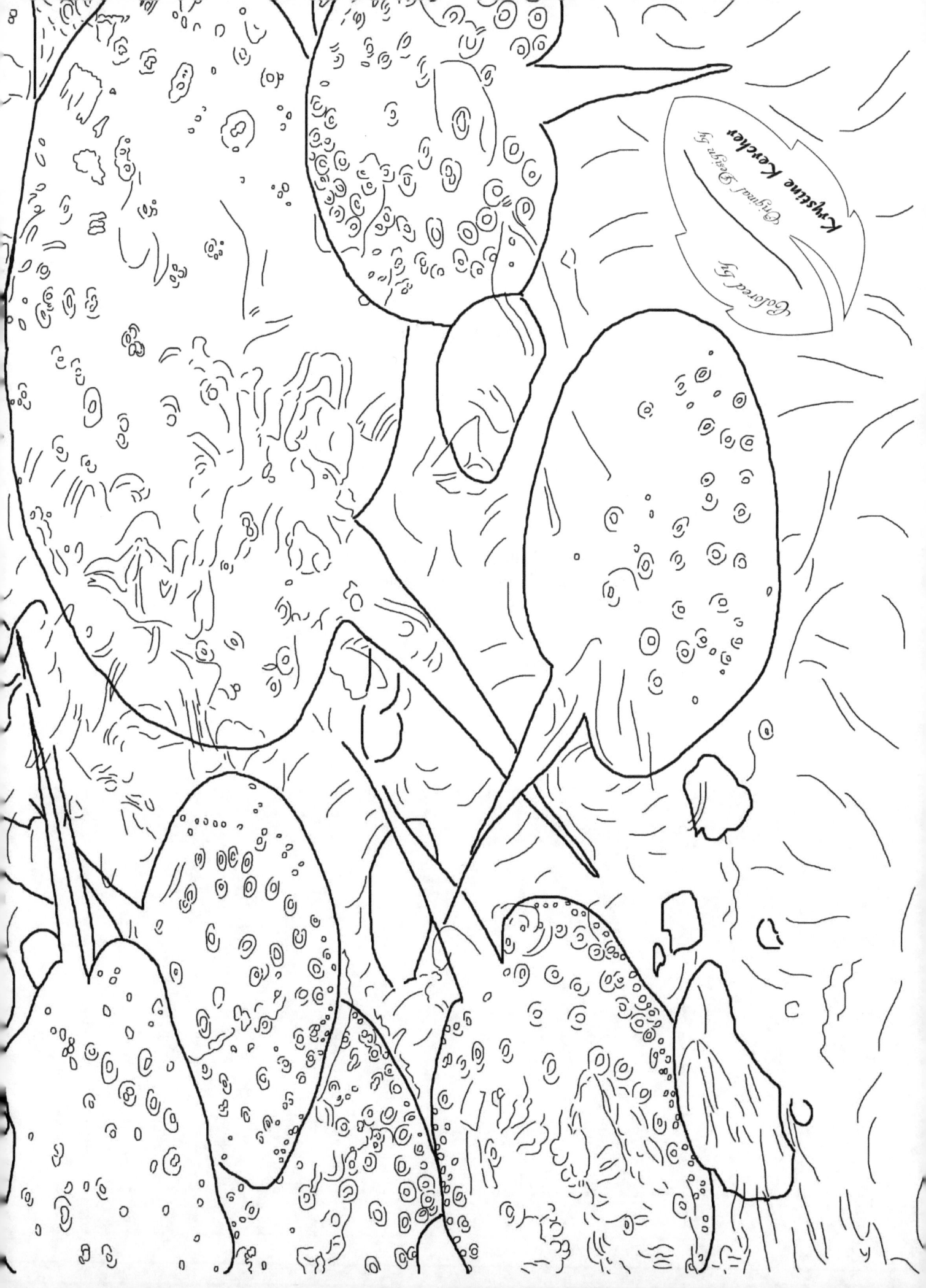

22 - Freshwater Stingrays

These freshwater rays from South America sport classy shades of gray with orange spots ringed in darker charcoal gray. They look really lovely against a bed of yellow sand.

One of the challenges this picture offers is in dealing with the highlights created by the light bouncing off the clear water.

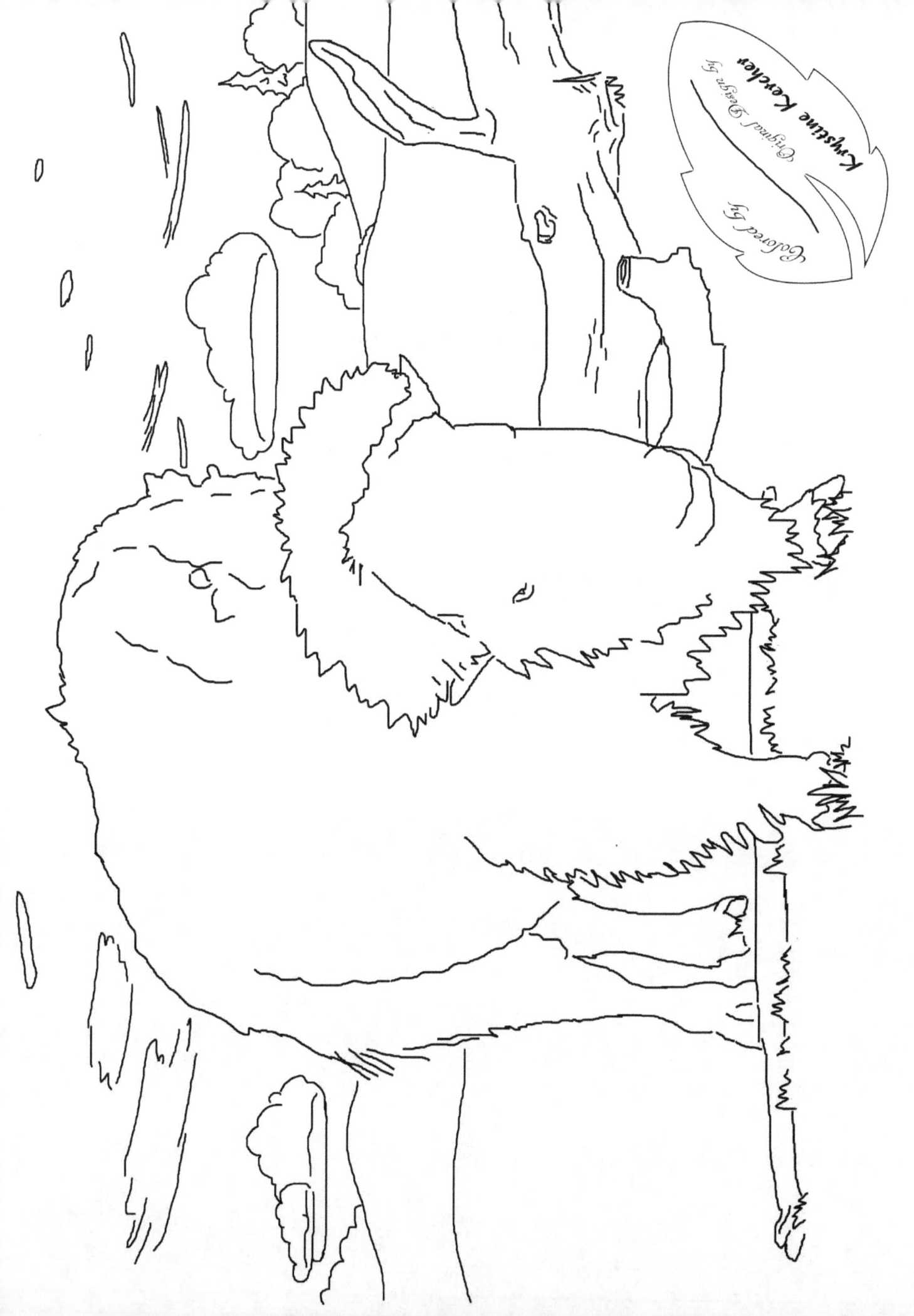

23 - American Bison

Shaggy American bison, also sometimes called buffalo, are among the largest animals at the zoo.

Herds of bison are still raised in parts of the western United States for meat and their warm shaggy skins.

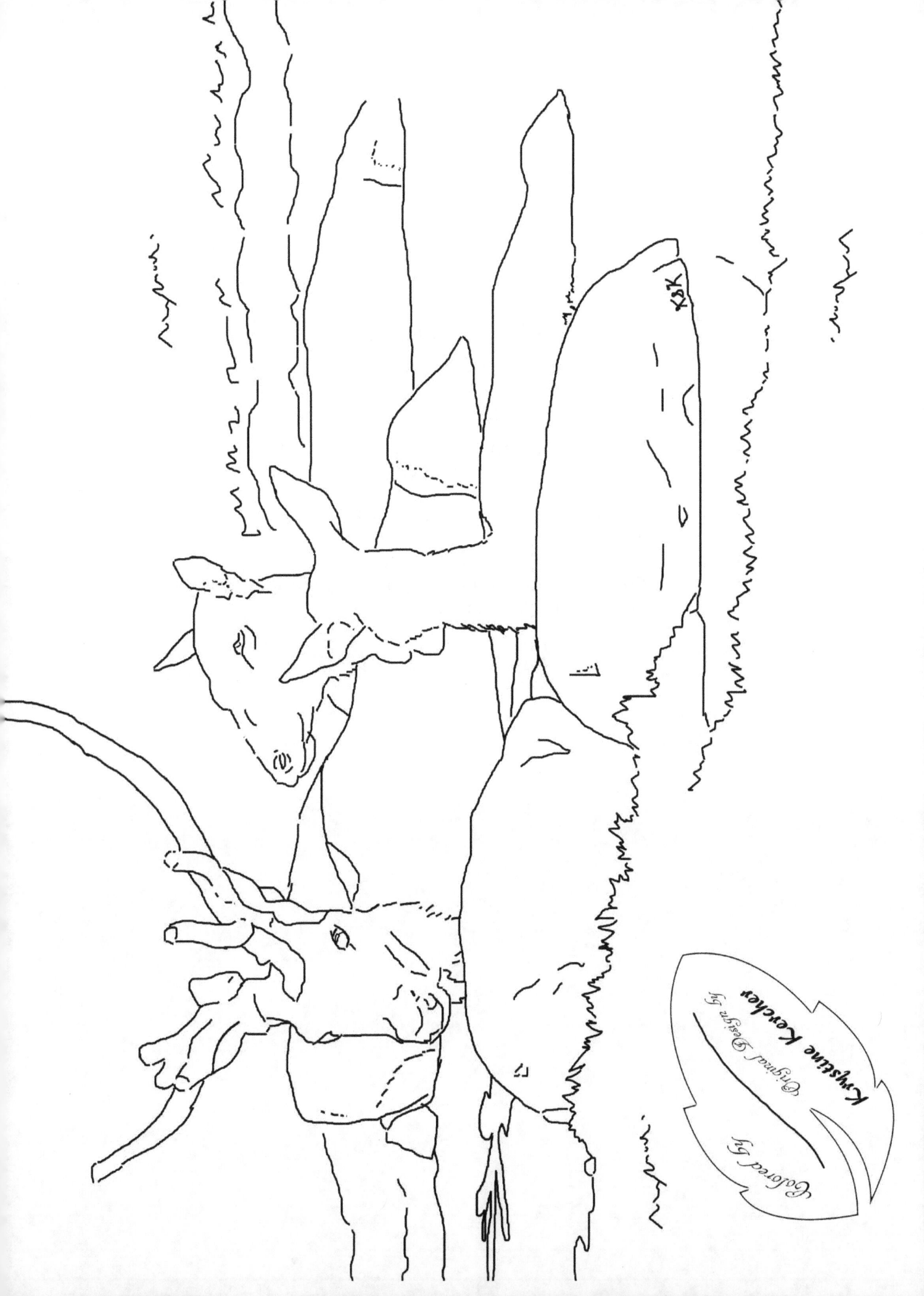

Colored by

Original Design by

Krystine Kercher

24 - Herd of Elk

This herd of elk decided they'd rather stand in the pond than deal with all the insects!

Male elk are called bulls. Female elk are called cows.

Coloring tip: the water of this pond was covered in a mat of bright green algae.

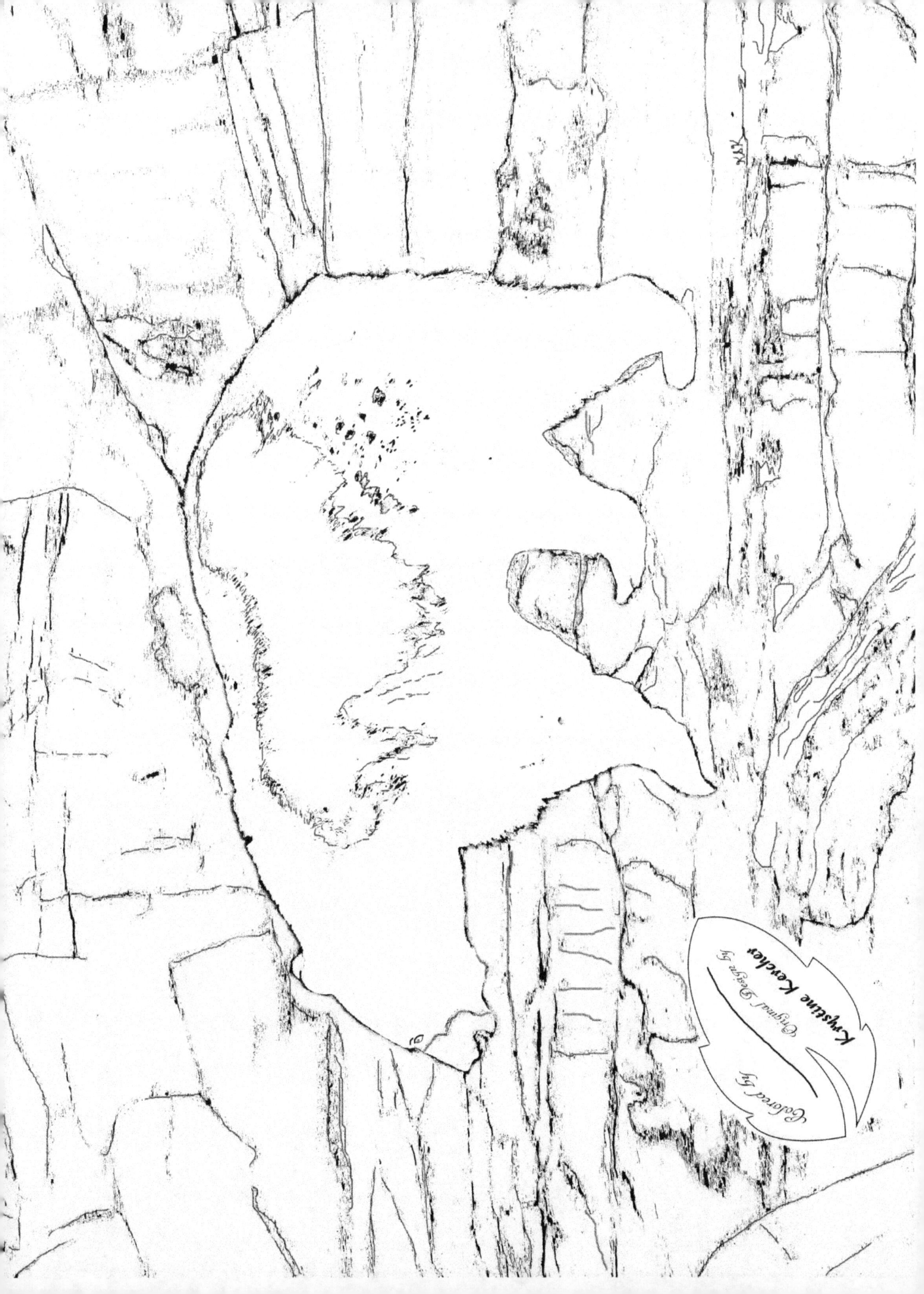

25 – Black Bear

This black bear was busy getting his exercise when I took his picture!

Artist's note: I've used a slightly different technique to create this design, and included some grayscale texturing to help give definition to the rocks in this exhibit. The outlined area on the bear's back is where the sunshine created highlights on his glossy, brown-black fur.

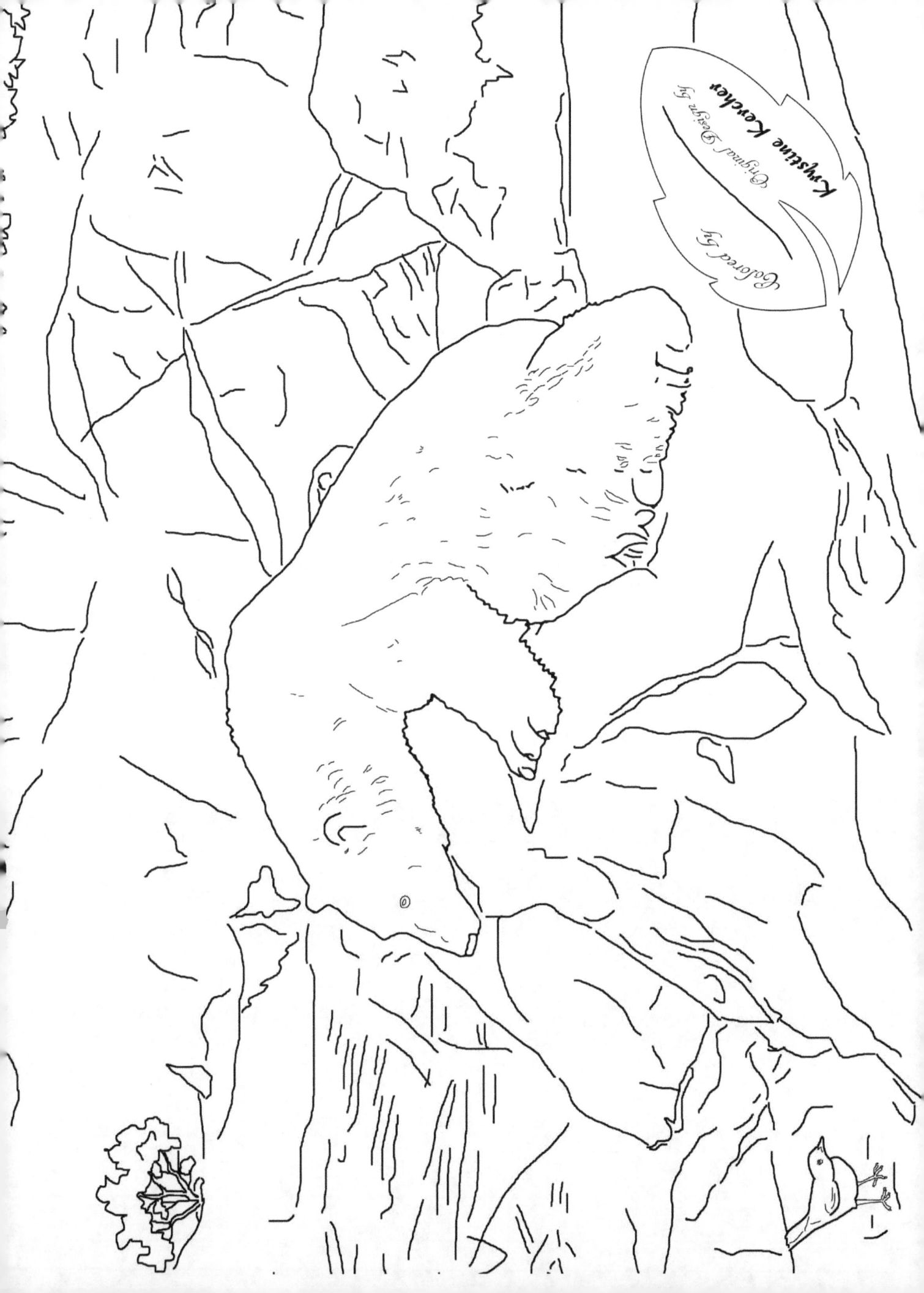

26 – Polar Bear

Polar bears live in the Arctic Circle, and like to hunt for seals out on the sea ice.

The day I took the photo for this design was chilly, but there wasn't any snow. I've added in some greenery and a small robin for brighter accent colors.

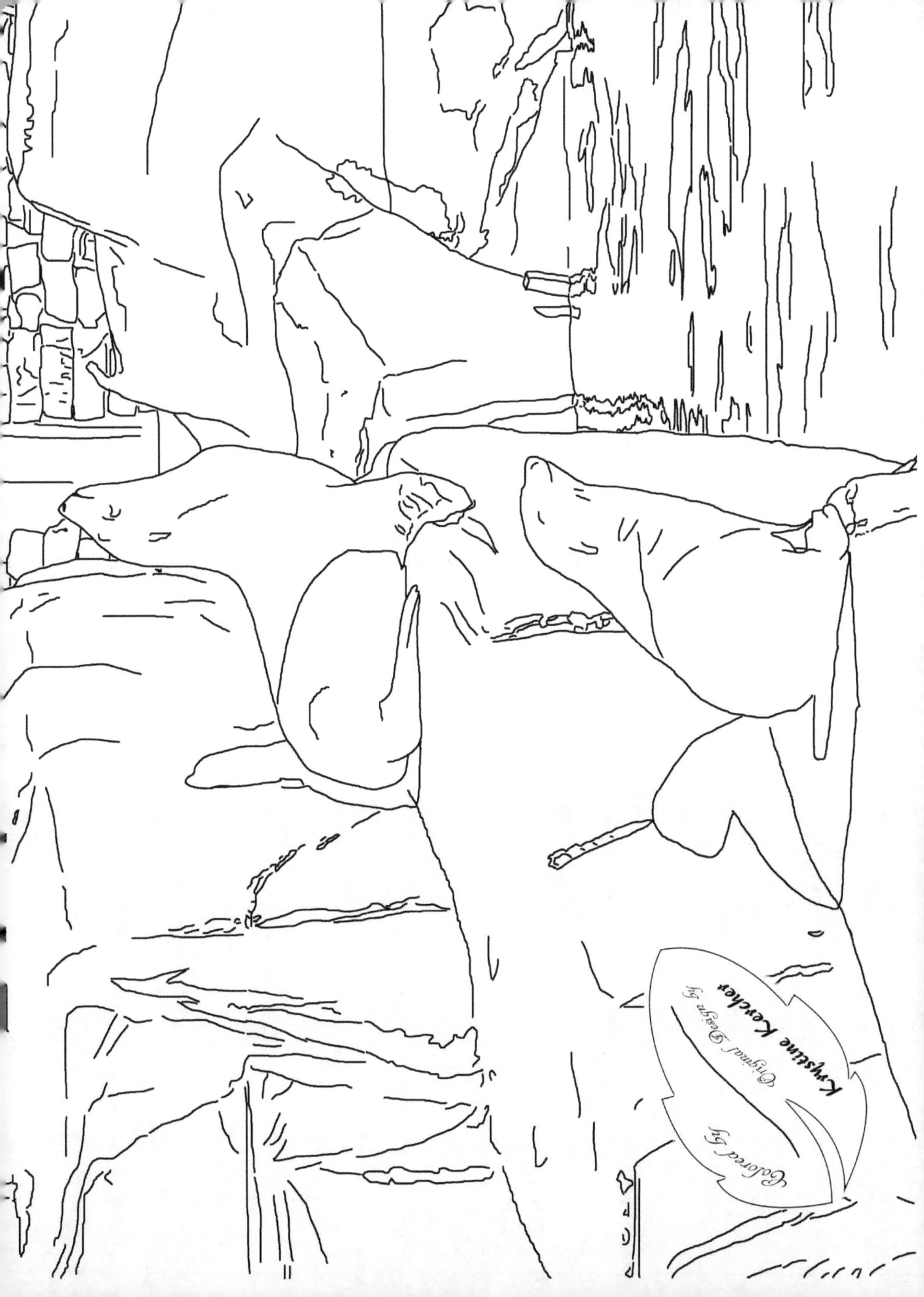

Original Design by
Krystine Kercher

Colored by

27 – Sea Lions

These sea lions are really the bright sunshine! In a moment, one of the sea lions will tease the other one into jumping into the pool. Down they'll go with a splash, and not come up again for minutes. I think they have toys they like to play with that stay at the bottom of the pool.

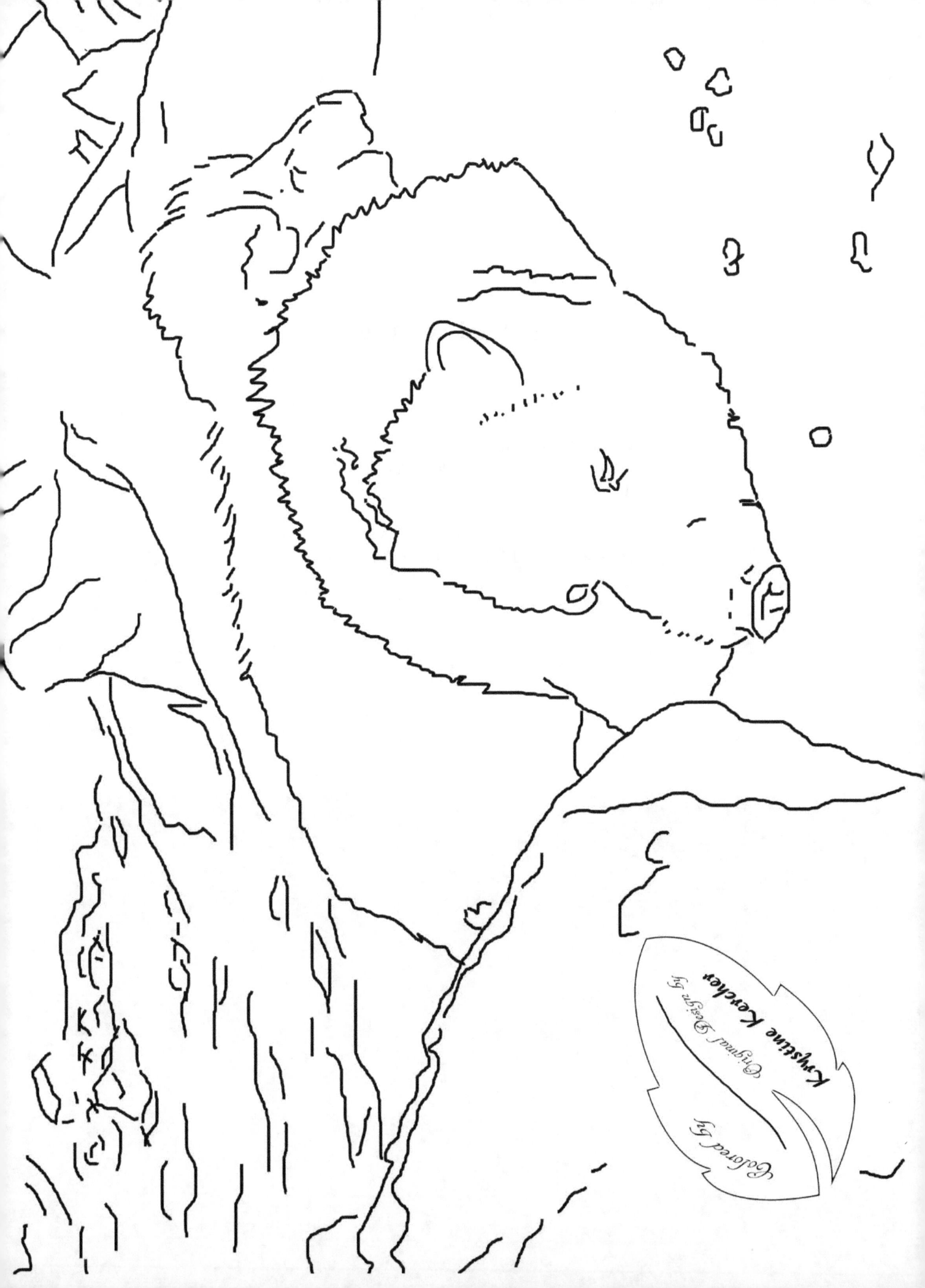

Original Design by
Krystine Kercher

Colored by

28 - Wild Peccaries

A peccary is a variety of wild pig found in the southwestern United States and down through Mexico.

Peccaries prefer habitat with thick brush, mud seeps, and lots of food for them to eat.

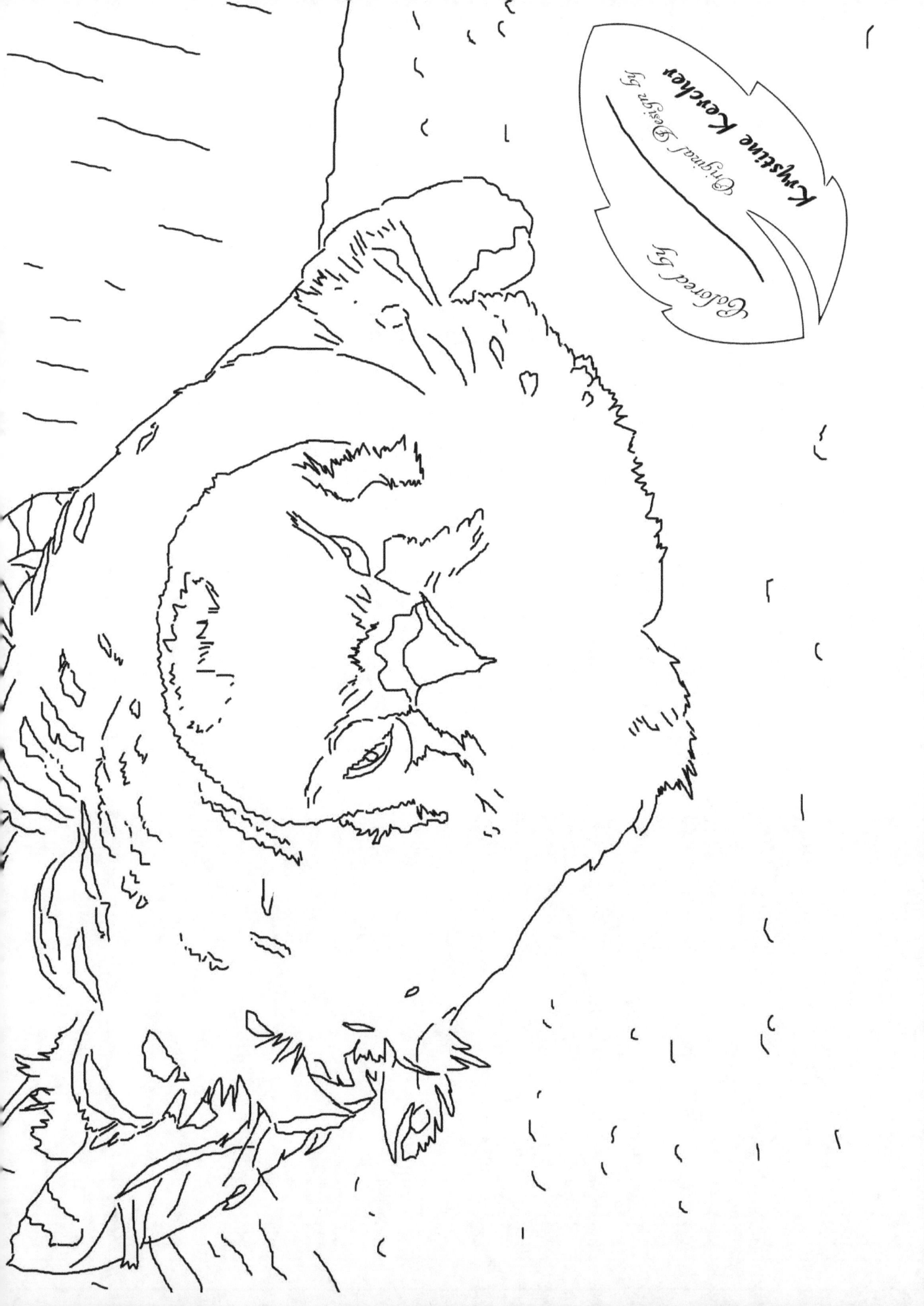

Krystine Kercher
Original Design by

Colored by

29 – Sleepy Kestrel

A kestrel is a small bird of prey. This female took a nap in a local nature center, guarded by its feisty mate.

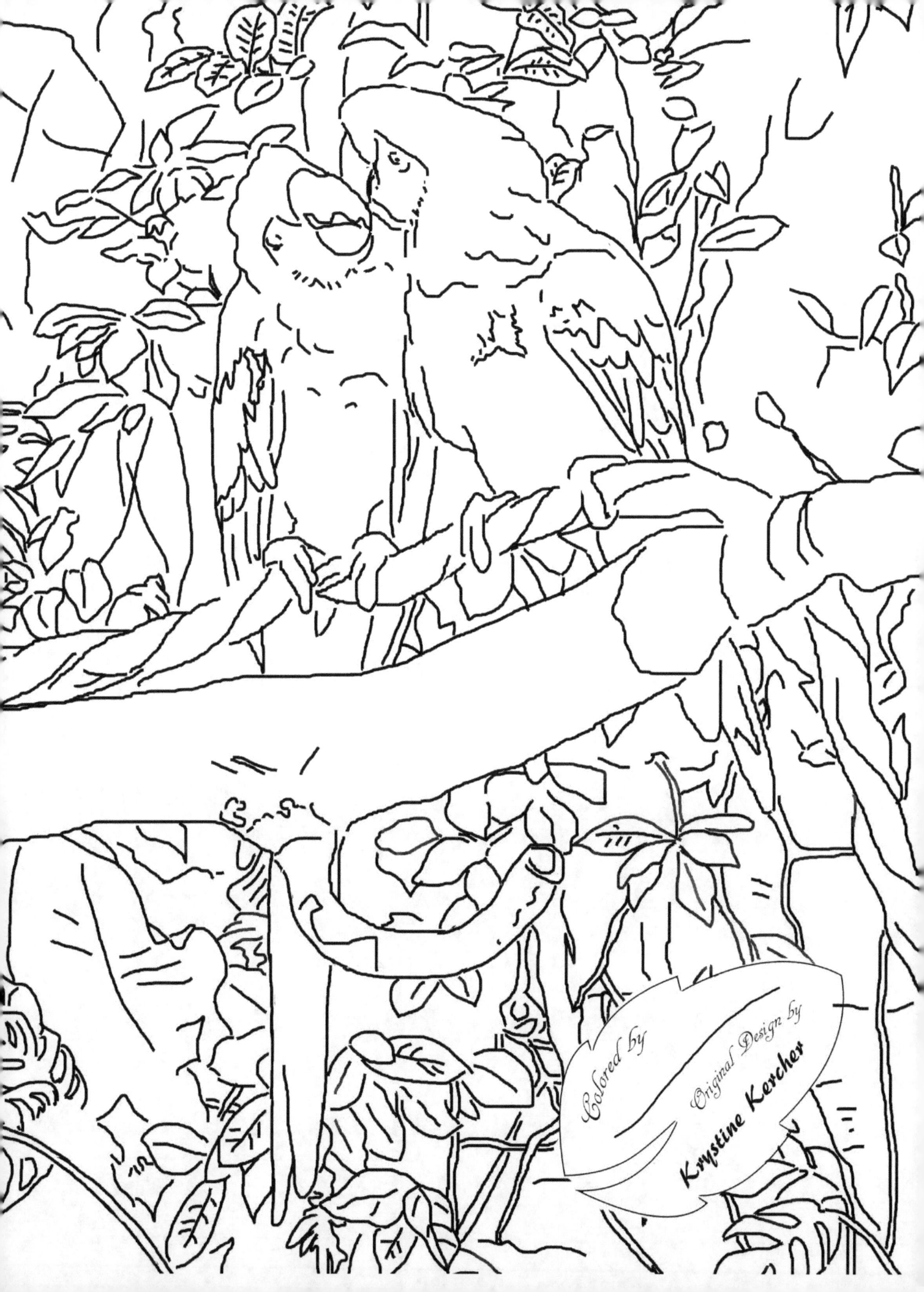

30 – Scarlet Macaws

These scarlet macaws are native to the rainforests of the Amazon in South America.

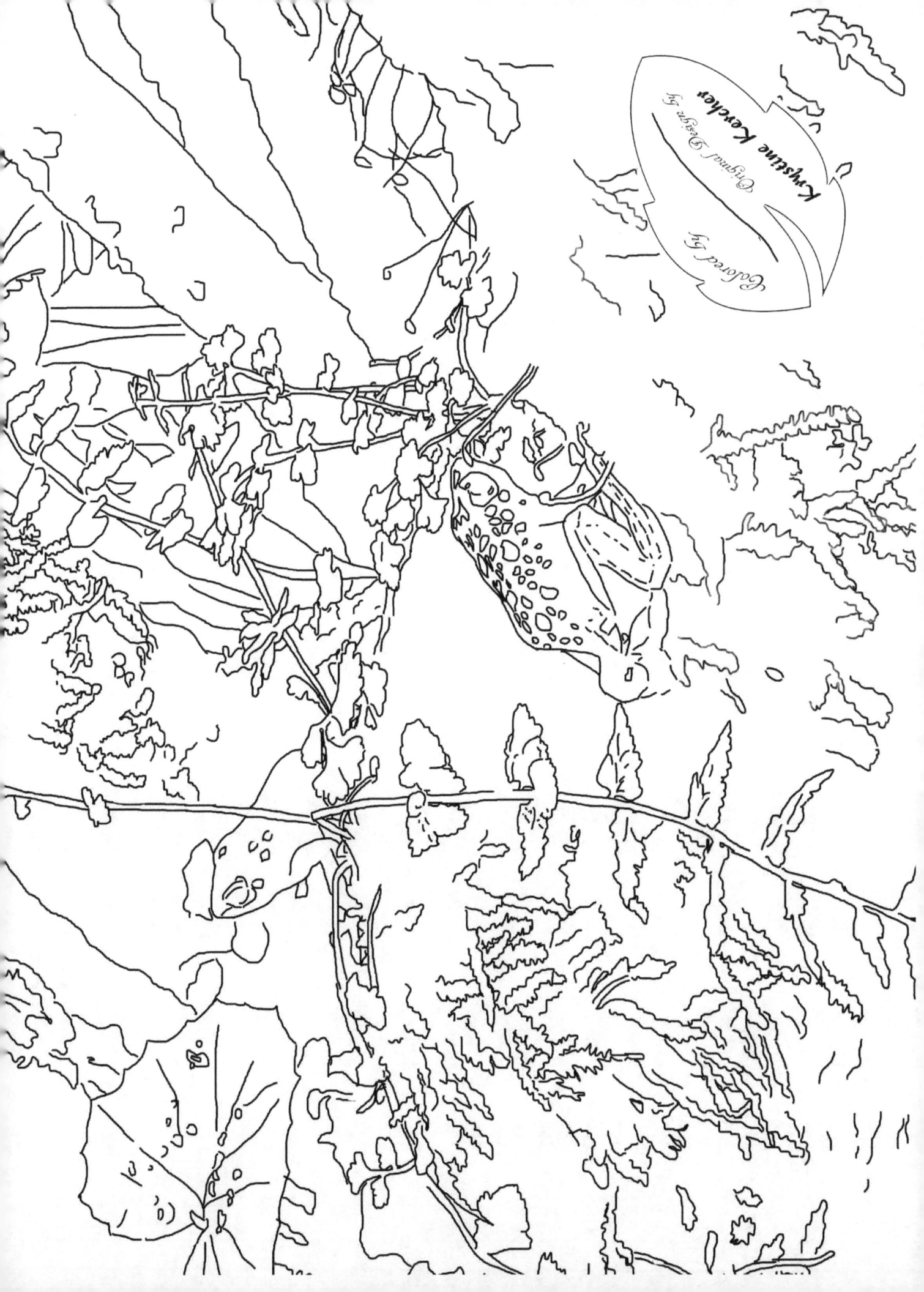

31 – Blue Dart Frogs

These frogs have gorgeous blue skin, but beware! They're poisonous to the touch. They're also native to the Amazon River Basin in South America.

Animals from Africa and the Middle East

Next, we're off to see animals from the forests and savannahs of Africa, and from the deserts of the Middle East.

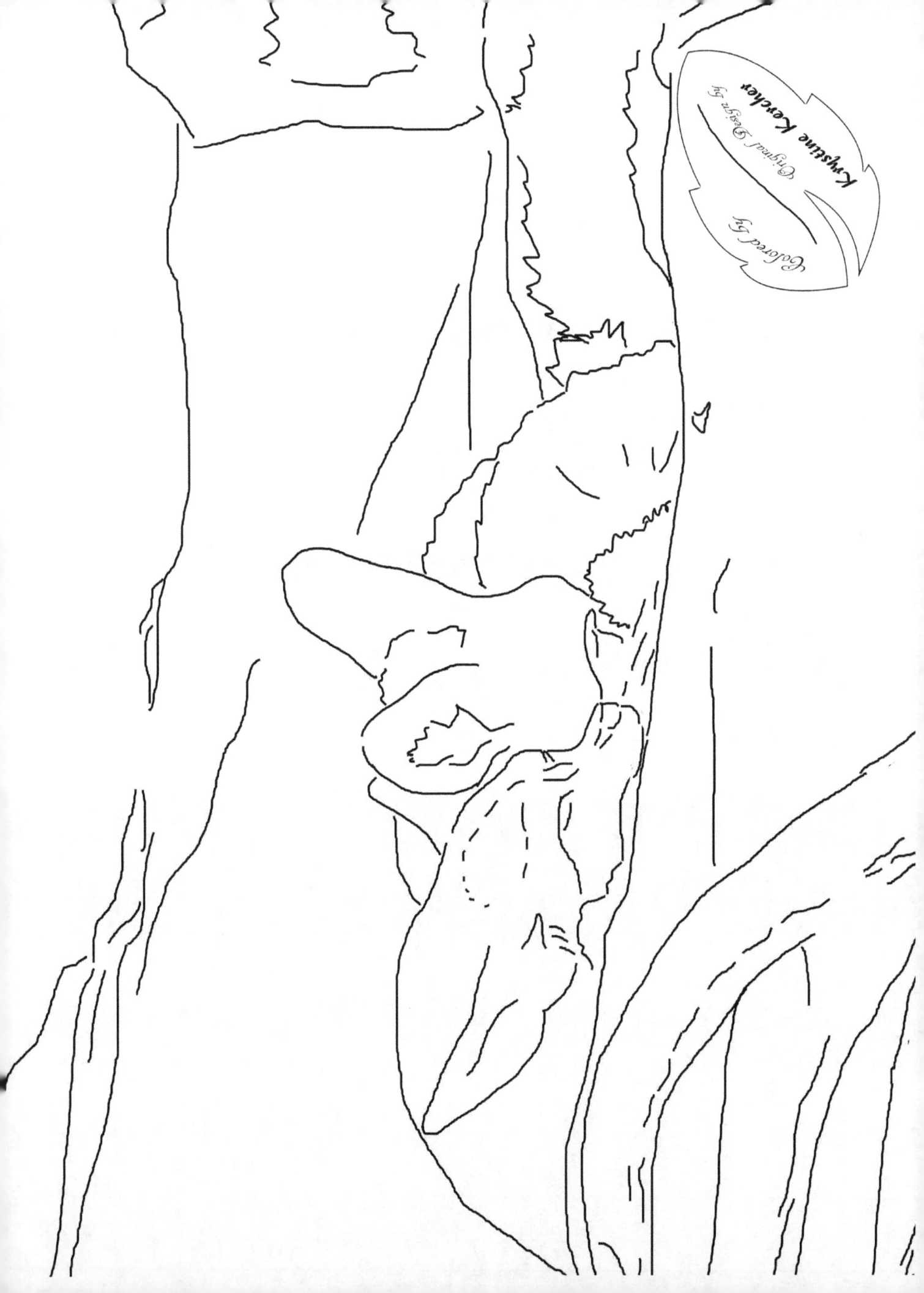

32 - Bat Eared Foxes

Bat eared foxes are nocturnal, which means they like to sleep during the day.

They live on the African savannah.

These foxes have black 'mask' markings on their faces.

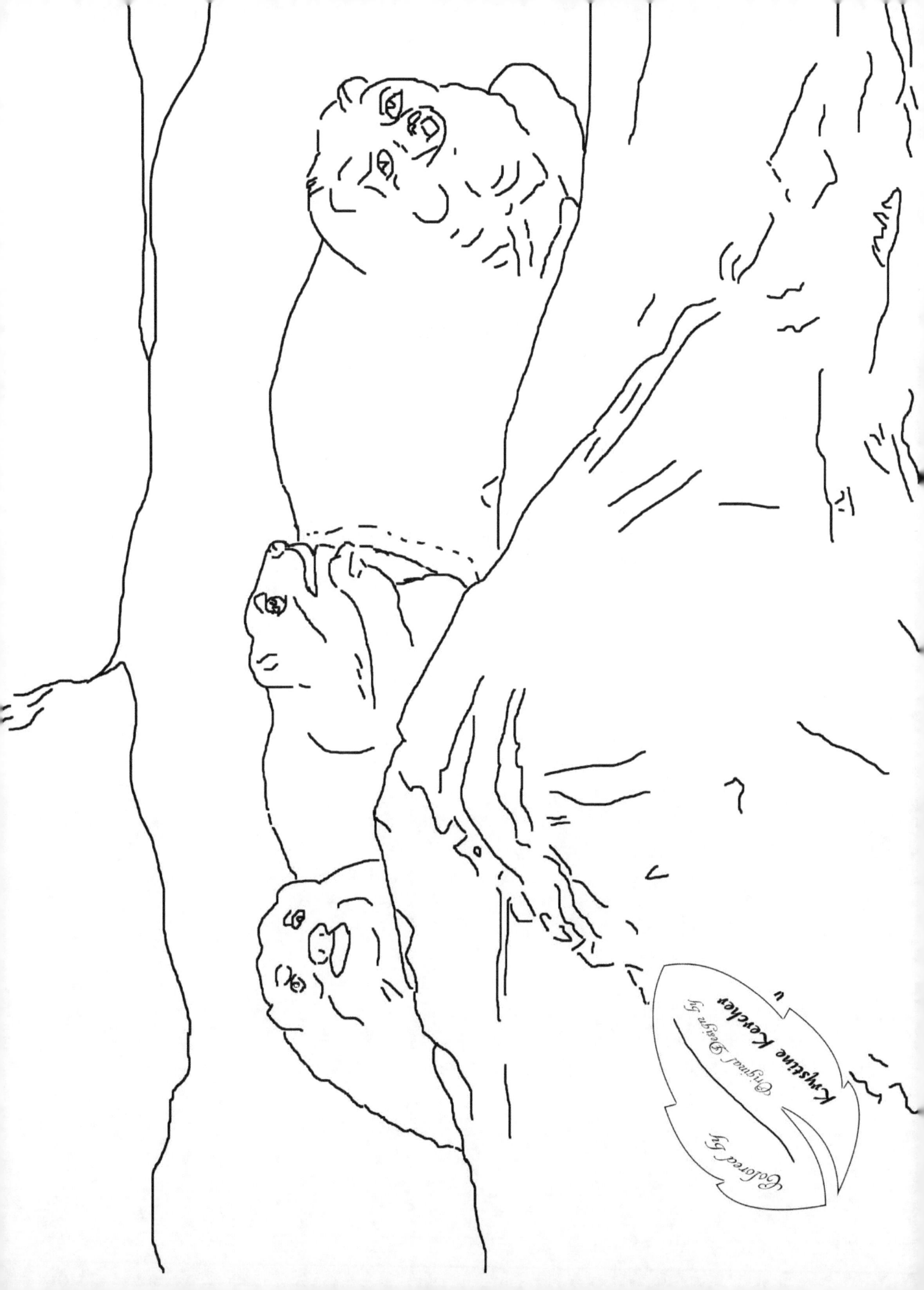

33 - Hyraxes

Hyraxes live in the Middle East, and are native to Israel, Jordan, and Lebanon.

These funny hyraxes look like they're enjoying a good gossip about the visitors to their exhibit at the zoo!

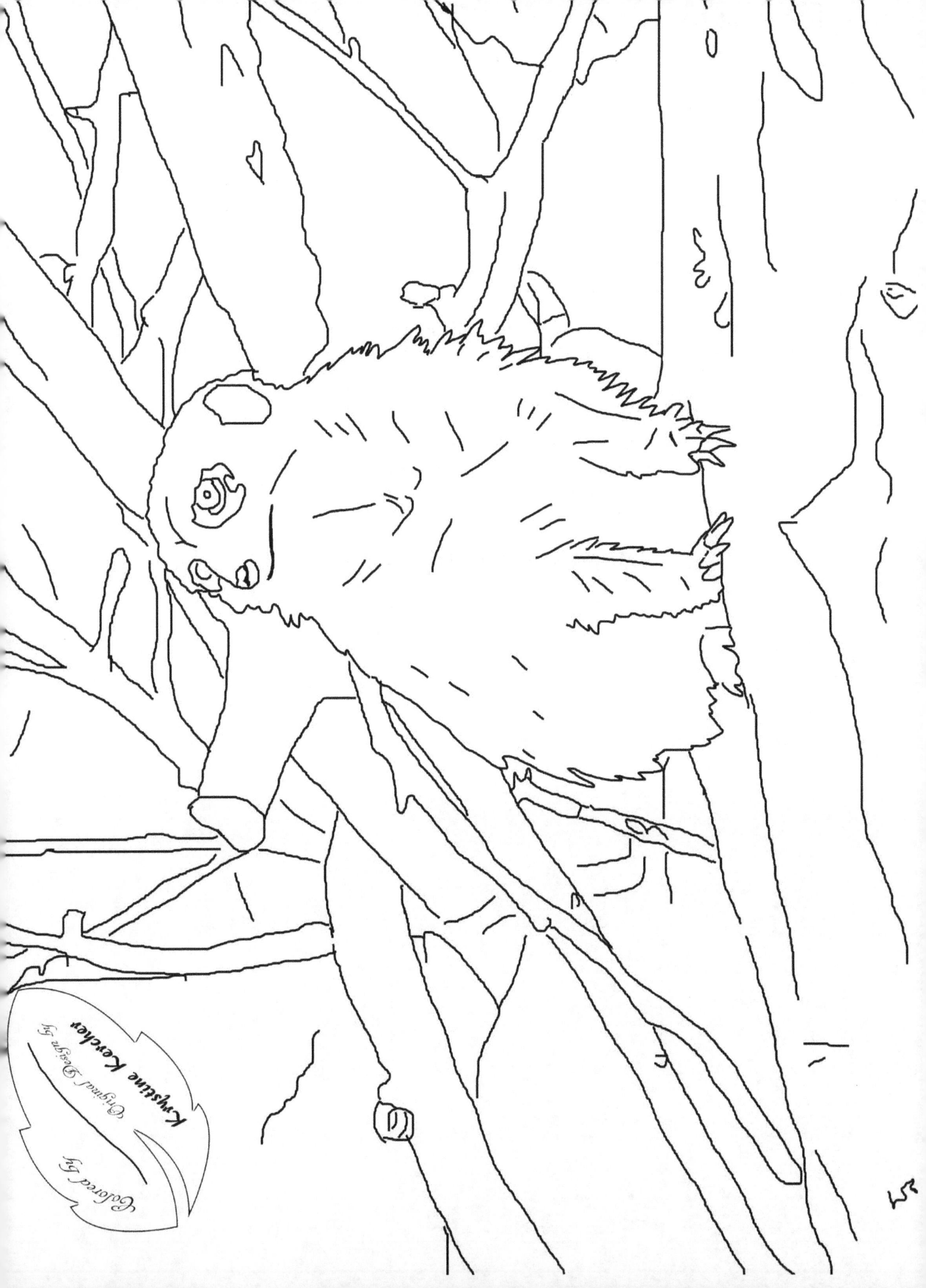

34 - Meerkat

Meerkats are social animals that live together in colonies on the African Savannah. They eat scorpions, small reptiles, and various types of insects.

Meerkats are relatives of the mongoose.

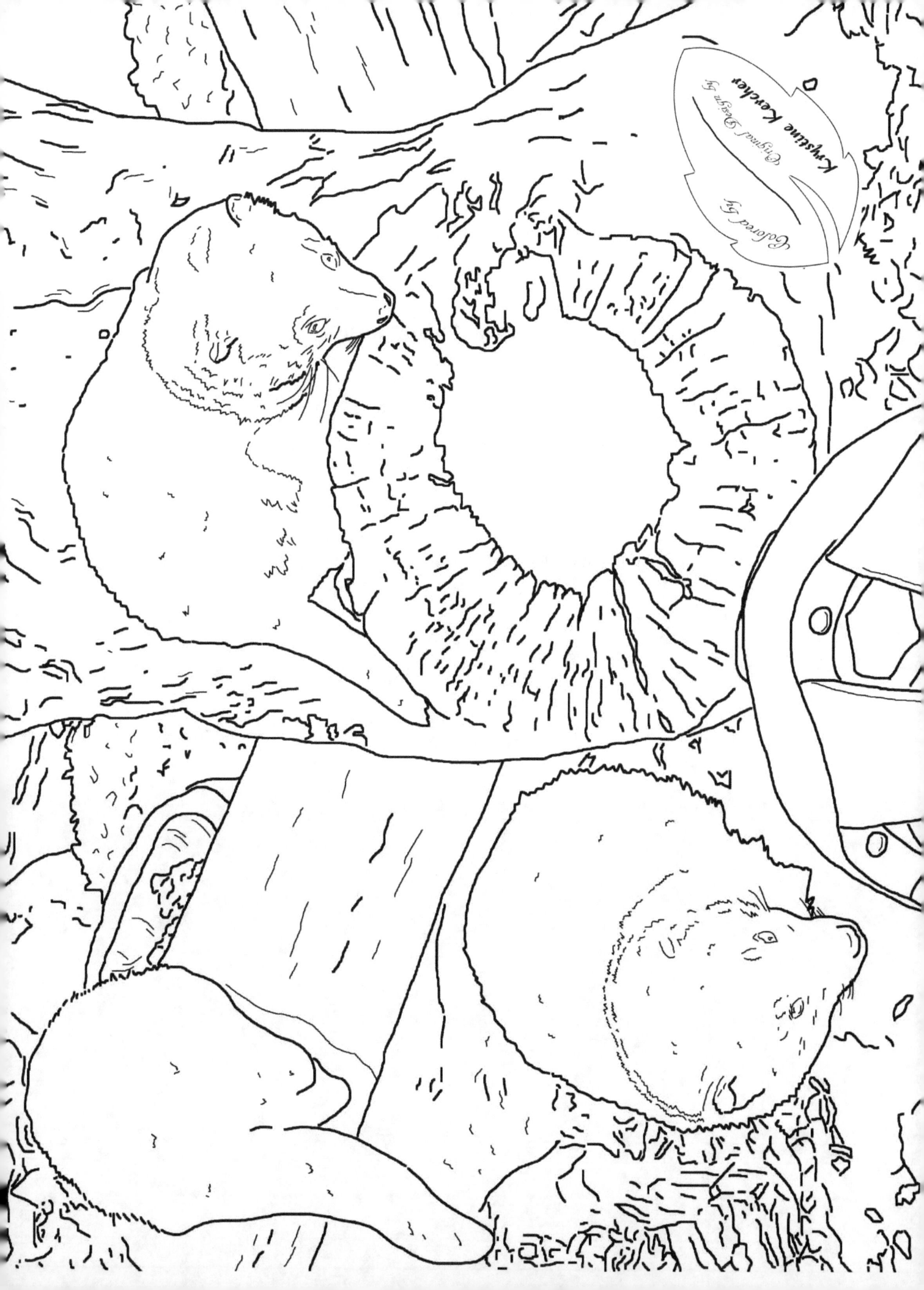

35 – Dwarf Mongoose

Dwarf mongooses are the smallest carnivores native to Africa. They live in packs and hunt insects and snakes.

Artist's note: they're also super stinking cute running around their exhibit!

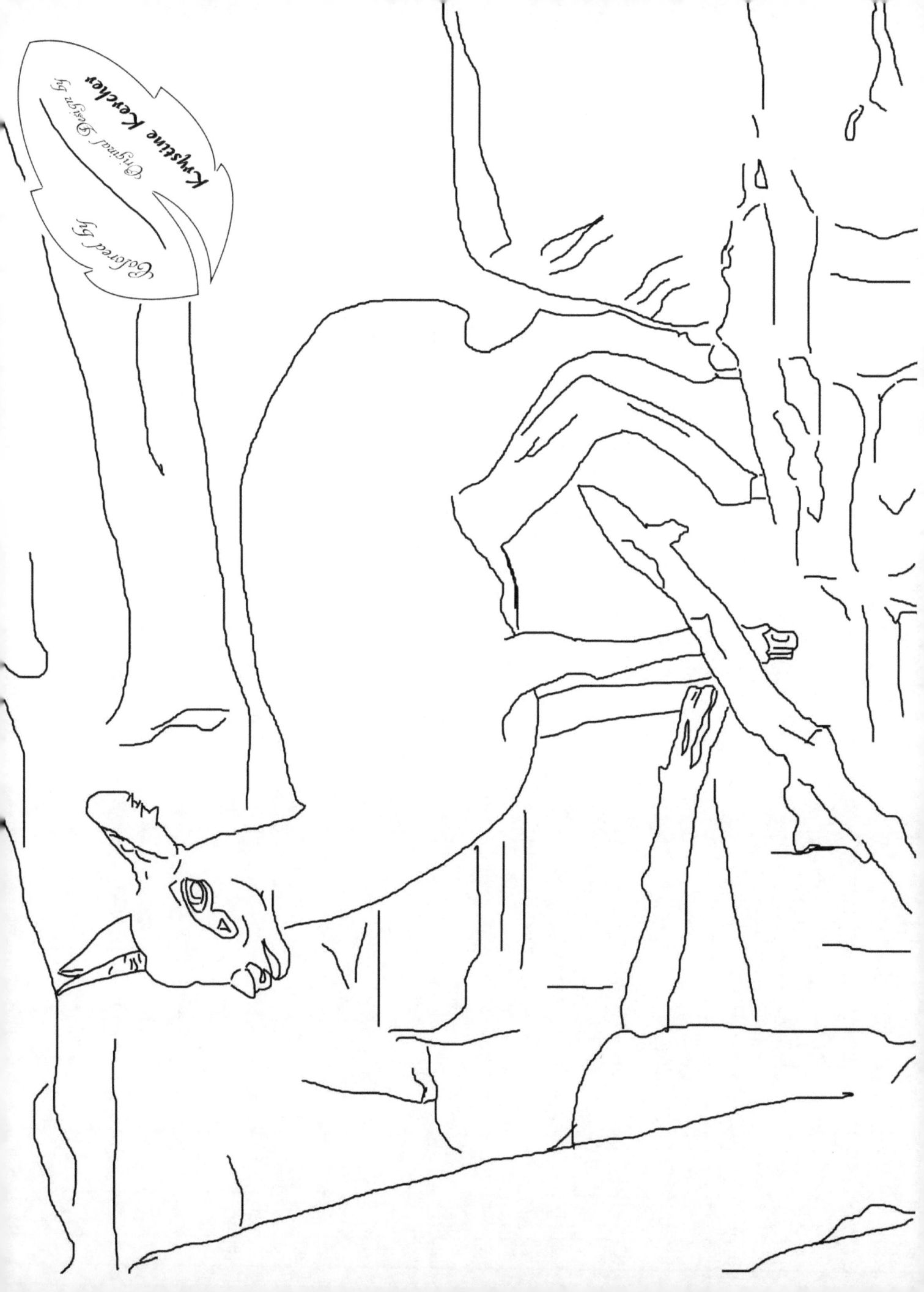

36 - Klipspringer

This is a klipspringer from Africa. A klipspringer is a type of antelope.

This particular klipspringer hangs out with the meerkats at the zoo.

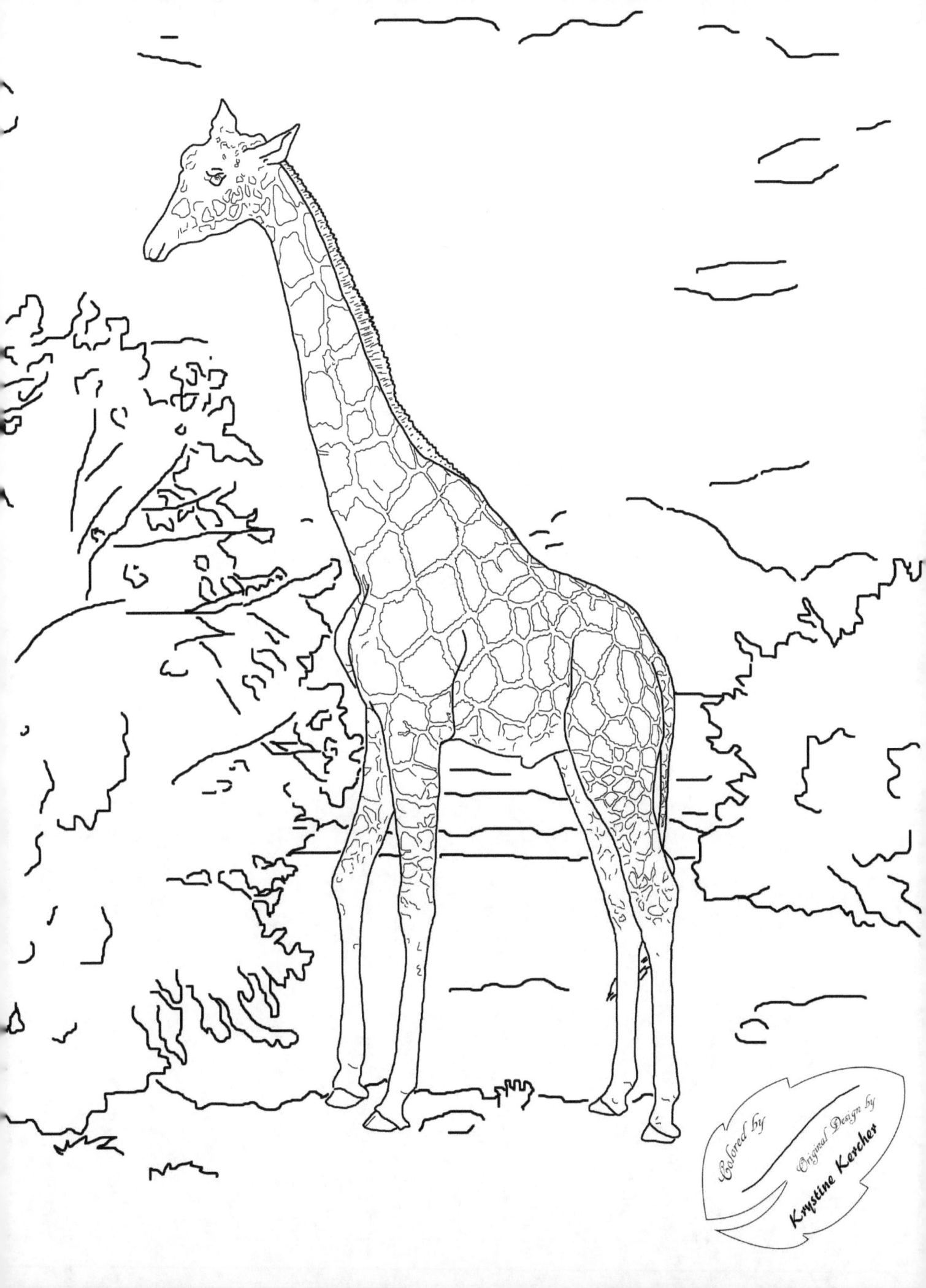

Colored by

Original Design by

Krystine Kercher

37 - Giraffe

Giraffes are herd animals that like to eat the leaves off tall trees. Their spots blend into the shadows beneath the trees, helping them hide from predators.

Artist's note: this is a young male giraffe which hasn't grown those knobby horns on the top of his head.

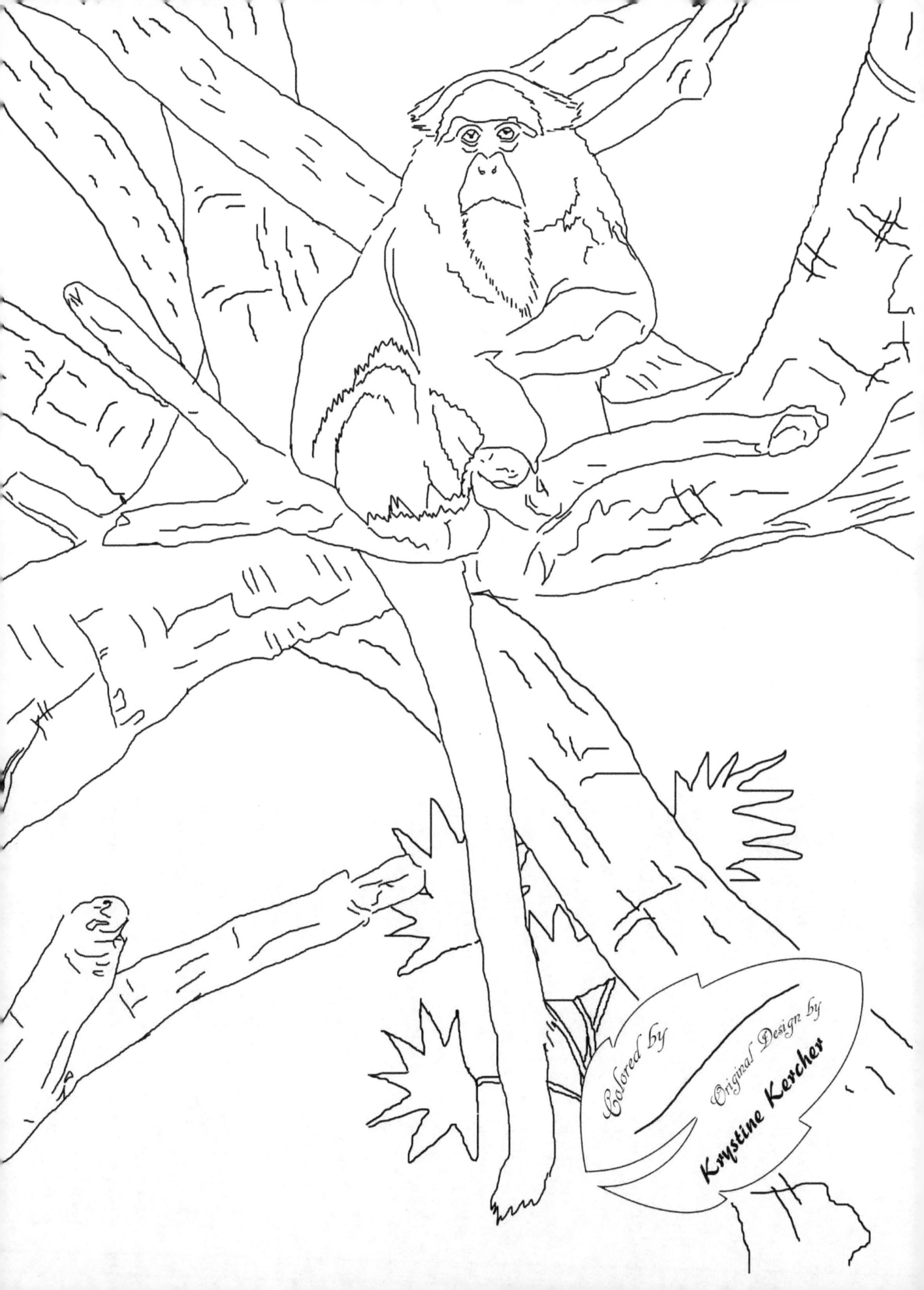

Colored by

Original Design by

Krystine Kercher

38 – De Brazza's Monkey

De Brazza's monkey is native to the wetlands of central Africa.

Artist's note: this particular monkey acted all embarrassed after I took his photo!

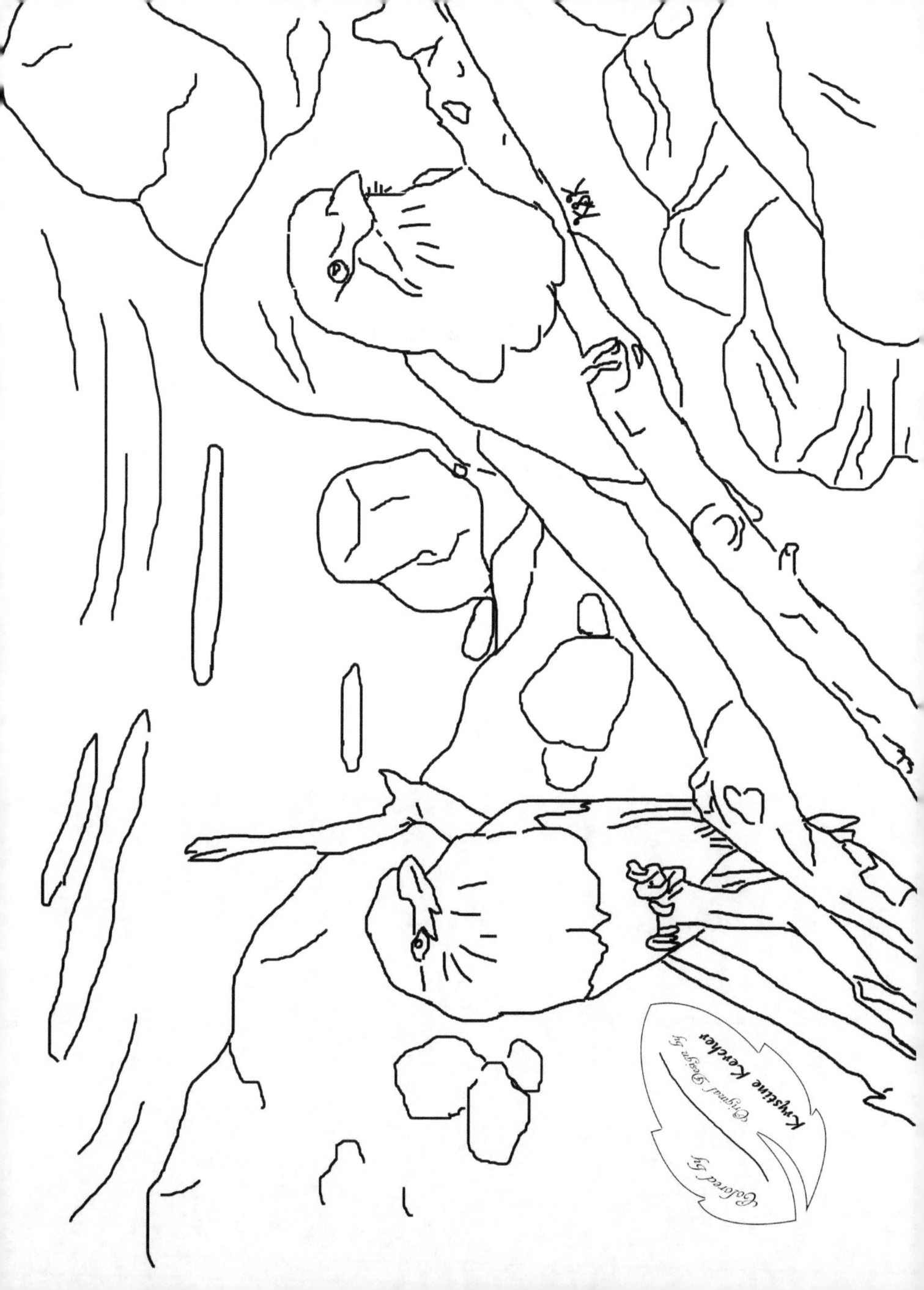

39 – Blue-Bellied Rollers

Artist's note: These birds from West Africa have the most gorgeous indigo blue feathers on their bellies! Their heads are cream-colored.

Animals from Asia and the South Pacific

Next, we're off to see animals from the forests and jungles of Asia and the islands of the South Pacific.

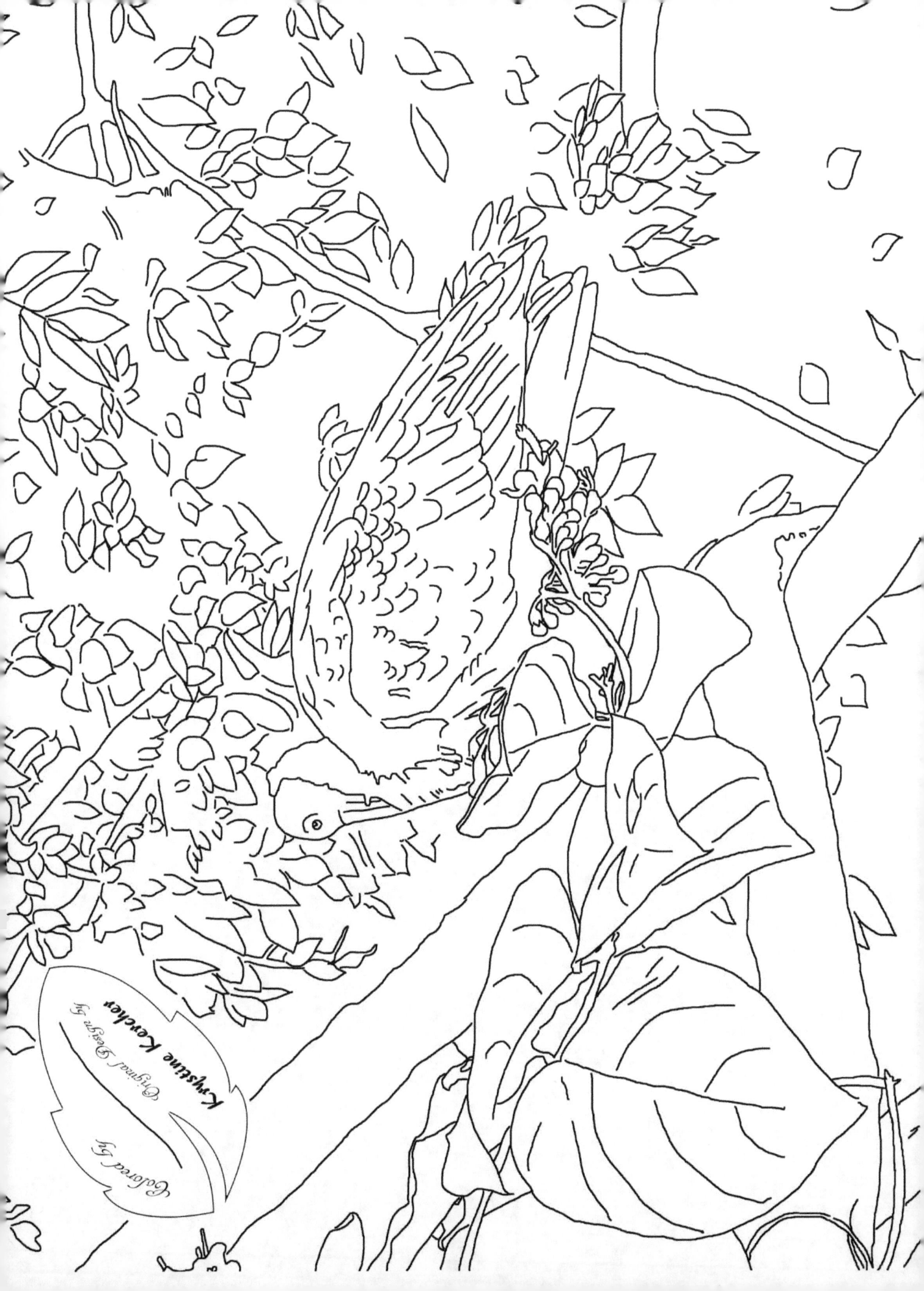

40 – Straw-Necked Ibis

This colorful ibis with iridescent feathers is found in Australia, New Guinea, and in part of Indonesia.

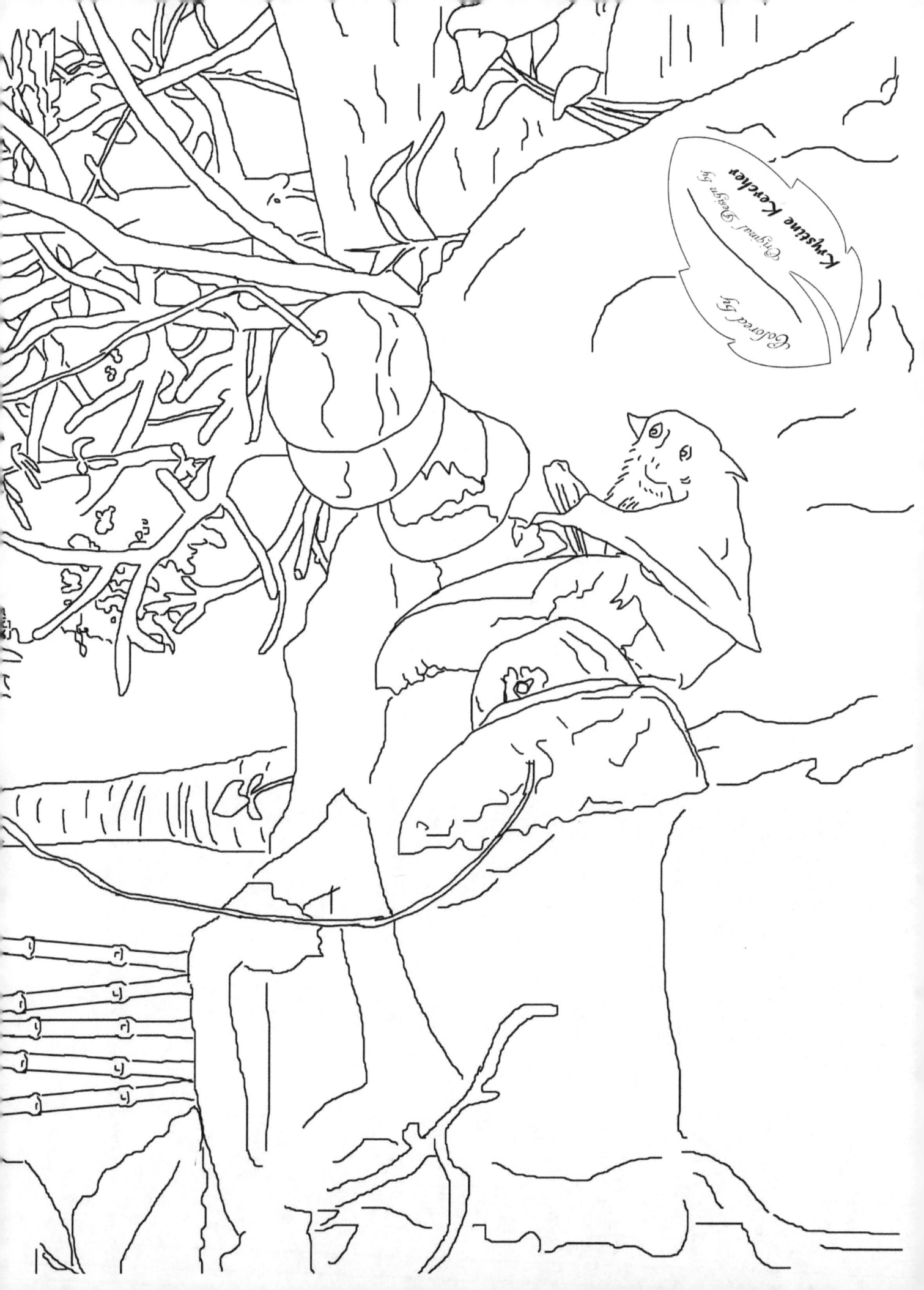

41– Fruit Bat

Fruit bats are found across Southeast Asia and the Pacific islands.

While this particular bat prefers fruit, other types of bats eat nectar, moths and other insects, and even fresh blood.

Bats are mostly nocturnal.

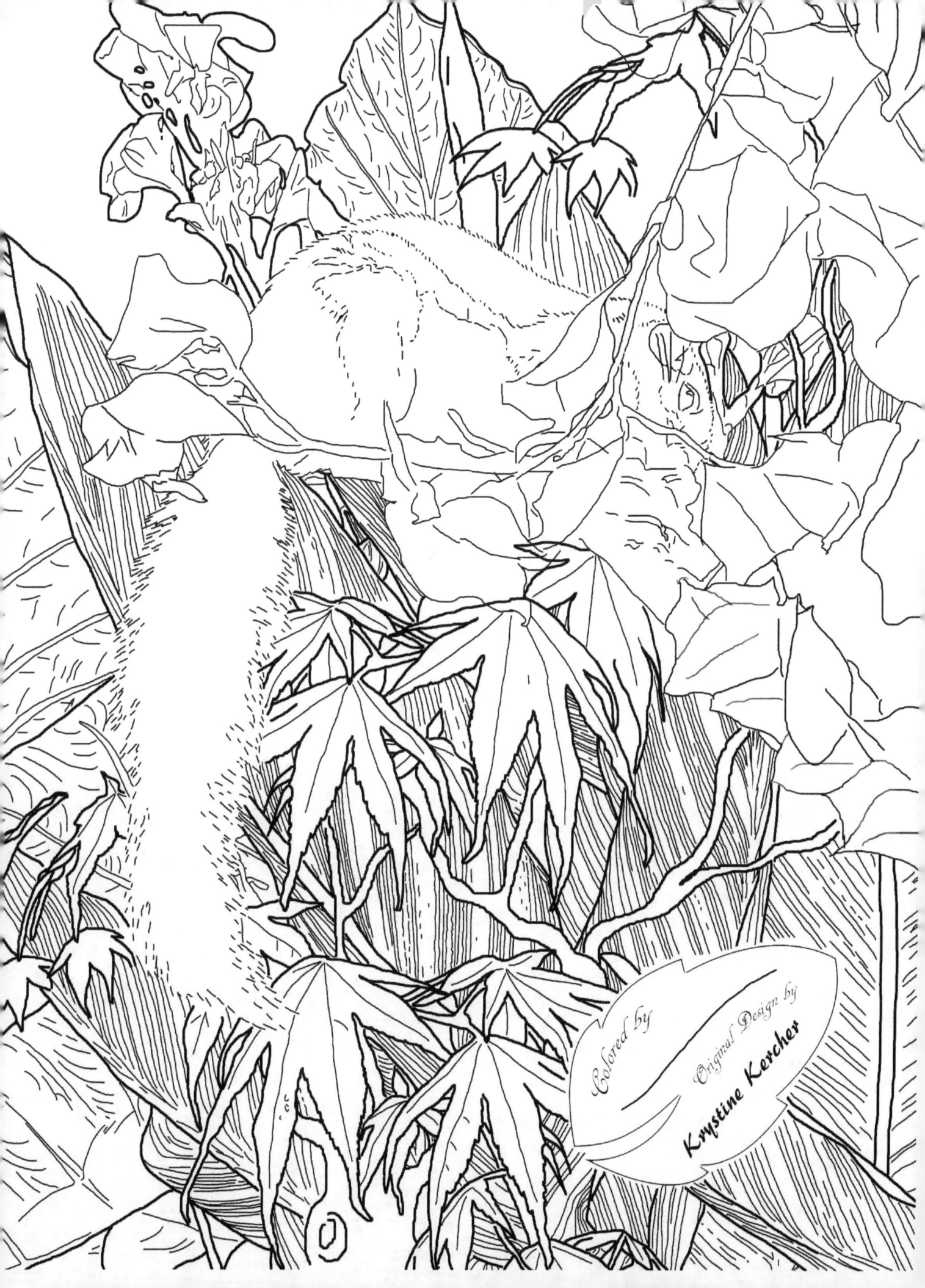

Colored by

Original Design by

Krystine Kercher

42– Prevost's Squirrel

This is a very colorful species of squirrel found in the forests of Malaysia.

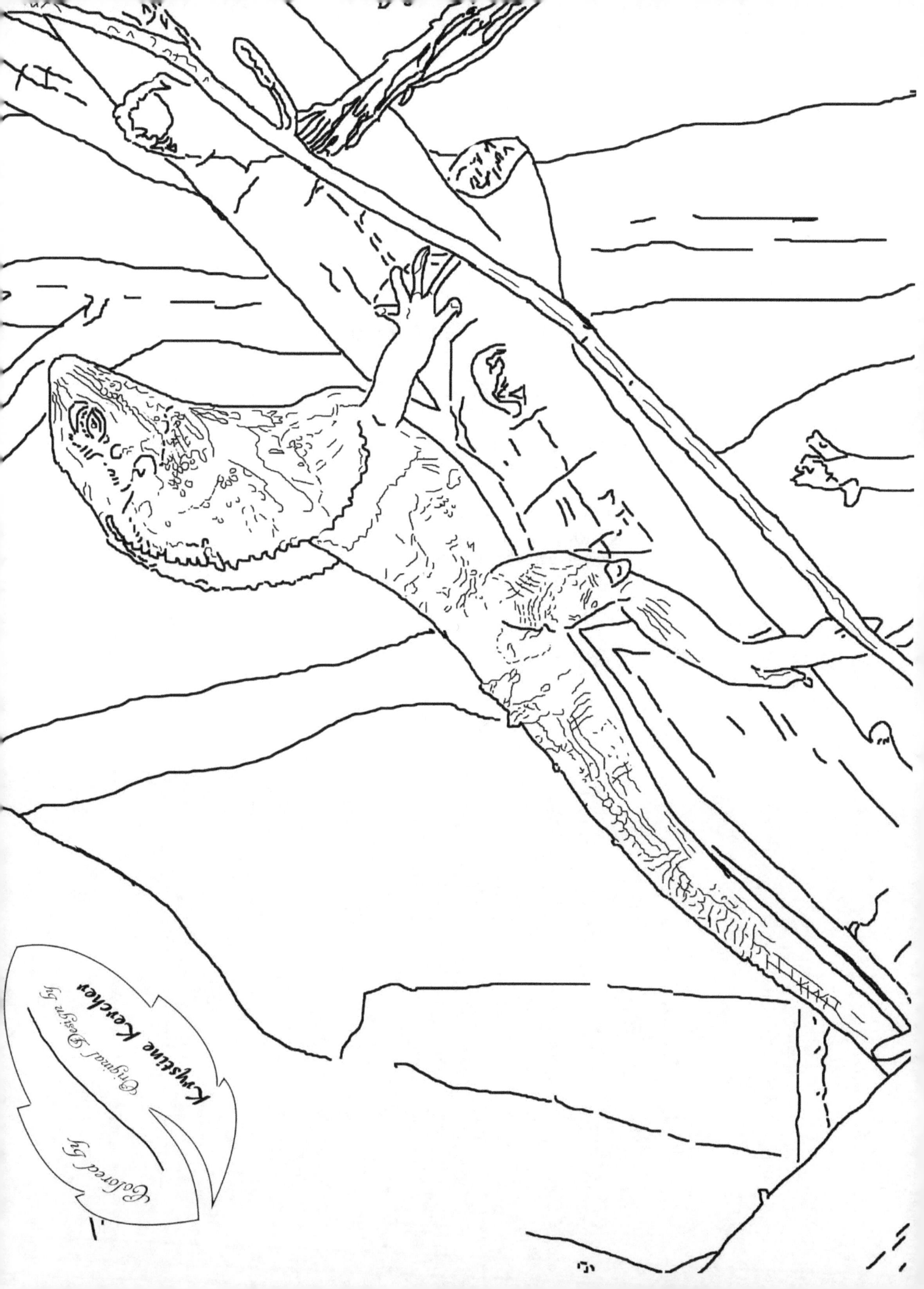

43– Frilled Lizard

Frilled lizards are native to northern Australia and southern New Guinea.

This lizard sports colorful frills on either side of the back of its head that open out to make it appear larger when threatened.

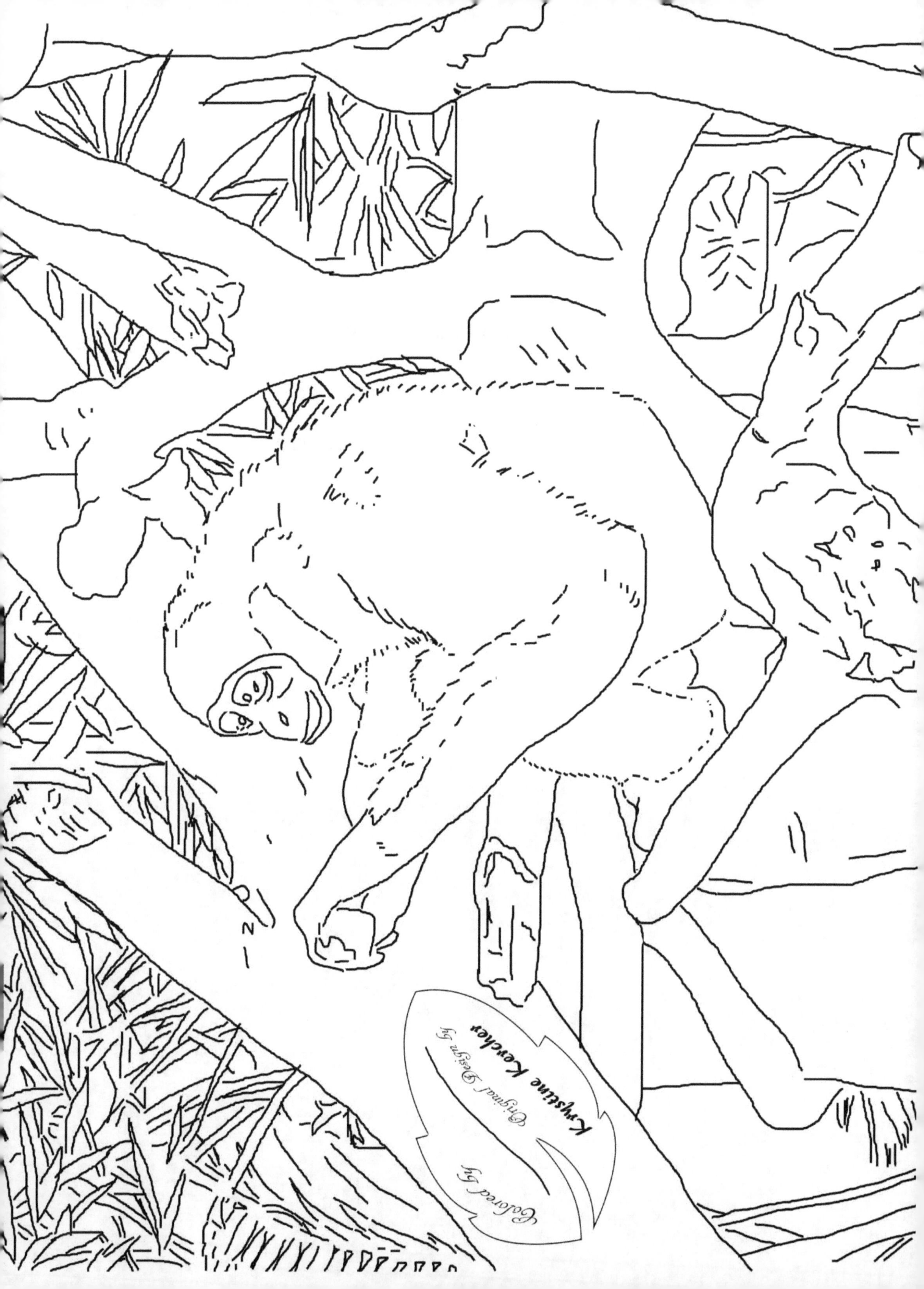

Kaystine Koncher
Original Design by

Colored by

44 - Gibbon Smiling

A gibbon is a relative of the monkey, and is fairly common in Southeast Asia from India to Indonesia.

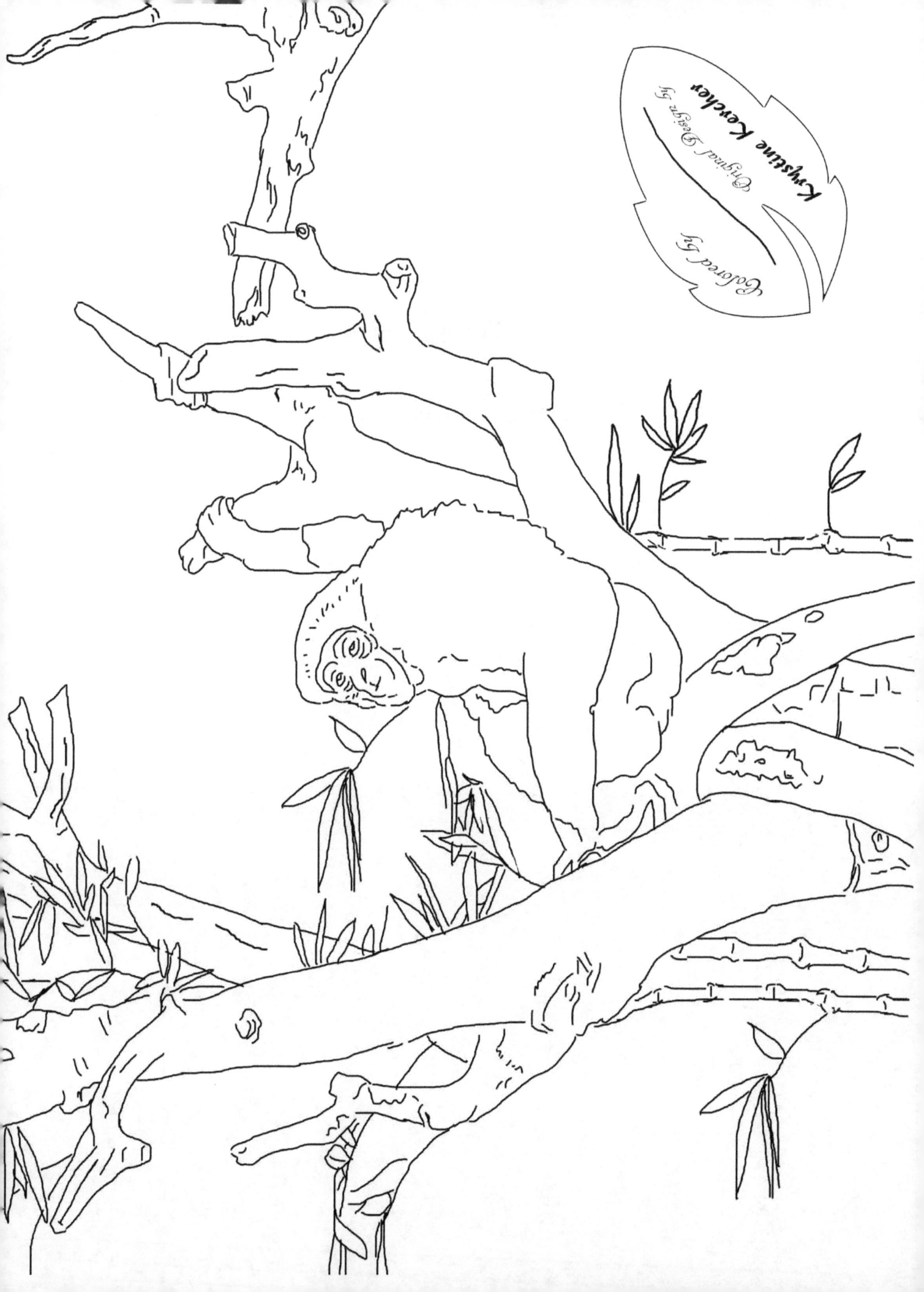

45 - Funny Gibbon

This gibbon had fun making faces at us.

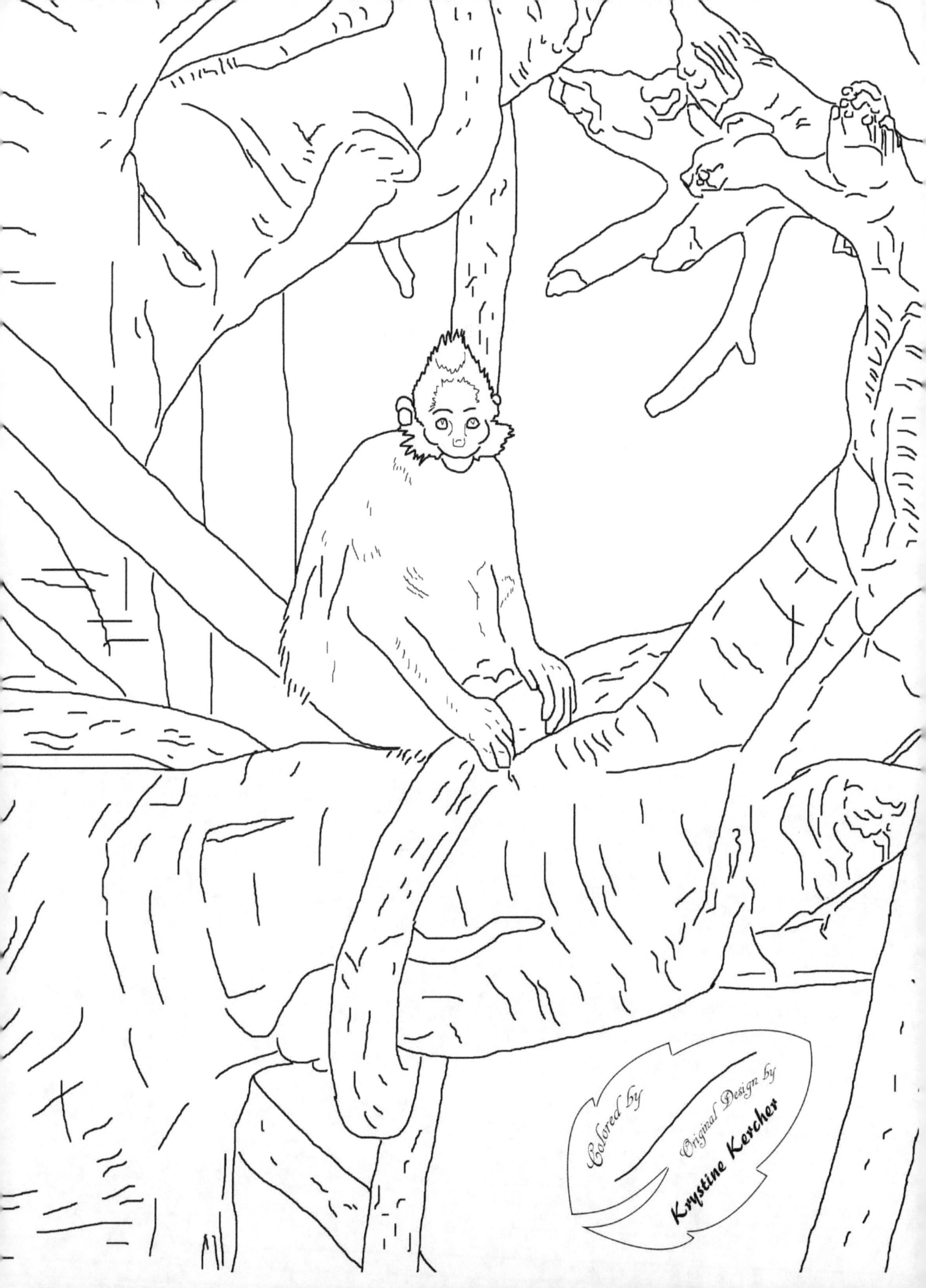

46 - Langur Monkey

Langur monkeys are also common in Southeast Asia.

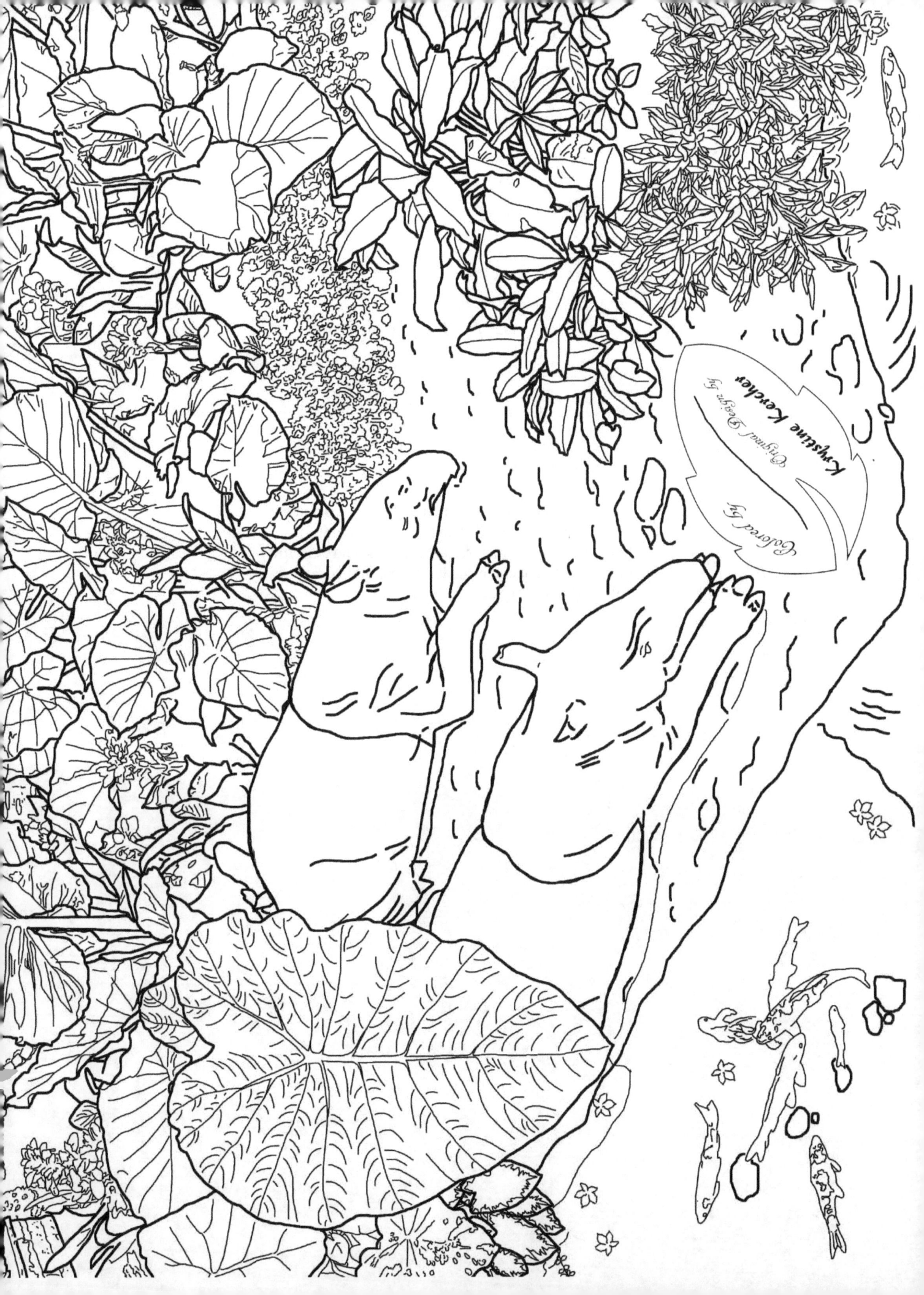

Colored by
Original Design by
Krystine Kercher

47 - Tapir

These black and white tapirs are from the rain forests of Malaysia.

Plants used in this design include large 'elephant ear' taro plants, canna lilies, banks of pinkish red begonias, Rubber plants, prayer plants, and colorful ornamental peppers in shades of red, orange, and yellow (bottom right).

One Last Design

I've included a bonus design of a yellow bird with a black head.

My research has unfortunately failed to turn up a name.

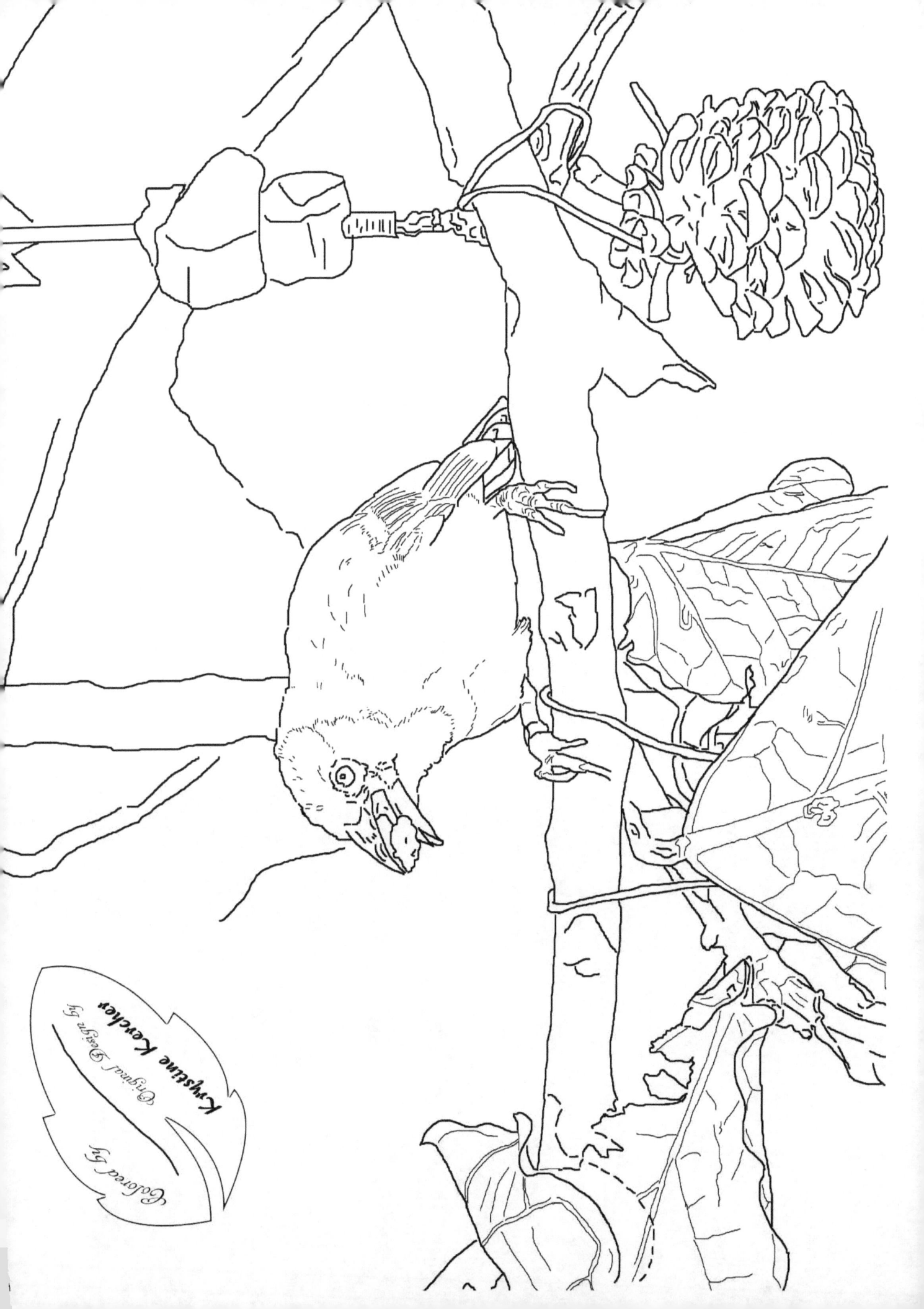